What Men Still Don't Know About Women, Relationships, and Love

What Men Still Don't Know About Women, Relationships, and Love

› By Herb Goldberg, Ph.D.

BARRICADE BOOKS

Fort Lee, New Jersey

Disclaimer: In all of the case histories cited and described, the author has used fictitious names and described traits not identifiable as those of any particular person or persons.

Published by Barricade Books, Inc.
185 Bridge Plaza North
Suite 308-A
Fort Lee, NJ 07024

www.barricadebooks.com

Library of Congress Cataloging-in-Publication Data
Goldberg, Herb, 1937-
    What men still don't know about women, relationships, and love / Herb
    Goldberg.
        p. cm.
    ISBN-13: 978-1-56980-330-1 (hardcover : alk. paper)
    ISBN-10: 1-56980-330-7 (hardcover : alk. paper)
    1. Men--Psychology. 2. Man-woman relationships. 3. Women--Psychology.
    I. Title.

HQ1090.G645 2007
306.7--dc22

                                                                    2007001211

First Printing
Manufactured in the United States of America

For Dr. George R. Bach, mentor and friend
1914–1986

Contents

Acknowledgments

In contrast to my earlier books, which seemed to materialize like magical events, *What Men Still Don't Know About Women, Relationships, and Love* took many years to complete, winding its way along and assuming numerous shapes and titles before finding its final form.

Almost from the book's beginning, Frychettya Randall was there to provide unwavering support, wisdom, and belief in the value of what I was writing. She encouraged me to include more concrete examples when the content became too abstract and, by her example, challenged me to consider the exceptions to the gender dynamics and behaviors being described.

So many things still needed to be pulled together when Marguery Lyvers began to work as my writing assistant two years ago. Bringing to bear fine organizational and computer skills, as well as her writing acumen, she worked patiently as I wrote and rewrote this book and sought to find the proper literary representation. After months of trial-and-error searching, I connected with Adam Chromy of Artists and Artisans, Inc. His enthusiasm and belief in the value of this book together with his out-of-the-box approach to agenting brought *What Men Still Don't Know About Women, Relationships, and Love* to another independent and iconoclastic force in the literary world: Carole Stuart and her company, Barricade Books, my publisher. I am grateful for both Adam and Carole's involvement.

It is doubtful that any of my books would have been written without the encouragement and guidance of my late mentor, Dr. George R. Bach. His pioneering work with issues of aggression, conflict resolution, and gender communication shaped much of my work throughout my career as a therapist, writer, and professor. By his example, he gave me the confidence to write with my own voice.

Finally, though I was born two months after he passed away, I have stood on the shoulders of one of the seminal figures of psychology, Alfred Adler. More than any of the pioneers of our field, he explored and wrote about the unconscious manifestations of power and gender conditioning. His ideas and core concerns opened the doors that I walked through and benefited from greatly.

In sum, the journey to the completion of this book was facilitated by many others, and resulted in the book you now hold in your hands. Please read, enjoy, and consider!

Introduction

The price for misreading and misinterpreting a woman has become extremely high; divorce battles, custody fights, poisonous interactions, accusations of abuse, incest, harassment, and even rape alongside the everyday unhappiness lead to a need to escape through self-destructive behaviors and addictions. It is "crunch time" for men today. Their personal isolation and dependency on women is greater than ever, while women's anger, withdrawal from relationships with men, and defensive sense of being victimized also are at a peak. In other words, what men still don't know about relationships may be destroying their lives.

The discussion, exploration, and understanding of male/female relationship issues have been stuck in the vicelike grip of embedded clichés, politically correct interpretations, and the romantic oversimplification of the complex issues of male-female miscommunication and psychologically defensive polarization.

On every level of contemporary life women are growing and emerging while men are shrinking and failing. Unknowingly, men have been undermined by their process and way of relating, which has damaged their ability to adapt to changes in their personal lives, bond with their children, relate intimately to women, and develop close friendships. Without a significant change in awareness, insight, and commitment, men will become increasingly toxic in their personal connections, resulting in painful isolation. They need the vision and solutions that *What Men Still Don't Know About Women, Relationships, and Love* provides in order to properly begin a deeper personal transformation.

It is true that men's socialization has damaged their interpersonal awareness, sensitivity, and capacity for personal, non–goal-oriented focus. Men's process or way of relating, unbeknownst to them, often alienates, frustrates, and infuriates women and their own children. These are dangerous times for men with relationship blind spots who lack awareness and understanding. Becoming a fully conscious, "personal" being is no longer a luxury for men; it is a dire necessity.

In today's times, men need specifics, not platitudes, lectures, simplistic advice, and politically correct moralizing. They need concrete personal maps, not general "how to" ideas that act like a temporary "feel good" pep talk. Men need information and interpretations beyond traditional, superficial, and misleading beliefs and advice about love and relationships and the usual lectures about how to treat a woman.

This book is a guide for men who are confused because they still don't know how to react correctly in their relationships with women. It is a book for all men. This book explores a woman's process—the deeper invisible, defensive elements that underlie and create her experience of relationships, as well as his counterpart process that produces blind spots, blocks, and vulnerabilities.

Is the Interpretation of Women Possible?

Writing a book on how to interpret and understand women is based on two assumptions. The first is that the way women relate to men is consistent, and the second is that most men experience women similarly in an intimate relationship.

The obvious questions arise. Can generalizations be valid? Doesn't generalizing perpetuate stereotypes? Haven't women changed significantly in the last few decades, so that general notions about them no longer apply?

The approach of this book is one of identifying and defining the deeper elements that shape women's relationship responses. While the external and visible content elements are varied in women, there are deeper elements that remain consistent and have not changed. If anything, they have become more entrenched. These are the elements that cause men to conclude, "Most women are . . . " in the same way women do when discussing men.

Women don't just experience things differently on a personal relationship level. They experience things directly opposite to men and their experience is not negotiable by men's reasoning. That is, women cannot be talked out of, convinced, or pushed into seeing things from a man's perspective, which men repeatedly try and fail to do. The man who does not understand how women translate their personal experience and what the limits of man-woman communication are, is a man whose personal life is destined to crumble, as he watches his best efforts at loving lead to less than naught.

What are these dynamic elements that haven't changed in the face of the massive cultural and social changes of women's liberation?

- In spite of feminism and women's increasing independence and economic viability, the man initiates the dating. It is still he who pursues and *acts* to make things happen while the woman *reacts* to his initiations.
- In spite of feminism and women's increasing autonomy and economic viability, their focus in relationships with men is still on commitment and closeness, just like men's focus continues to be sexual and on a woman's physical appearance. Not only have these dynamics not changed, but the emphasis on these "bottom line" aspects has intensified. Once women decide that commitment and closeness are not going to happen, unless they have another agenda, such as economic support, they withdraw from the relationship.
- Few women see themselves as equal players in the progression, ongoing experience, and deterioration of a love relationship. They continue to hold men

responsible for most of a relationship's problems and disappointments and often portray themselves as the victims of men's insensitivities, deficiencies, and abusiveness.

• Despite increasing economic viability, a man is still deemed attractive and sexy by a woman based mainly on what he does for a living and how successful he is at doing it. A man's ability to provide or his potential for taking responsibility determines her initial interest and attraction to him.

While much has changed culturally on the surface, these deeper elements of embedded gender process, or the *how* of men's and women's interactions and behavior in relationships, have not changed significantly.

While some men and women temporarily transcend the traditional obsessions of their gender, few can maintain any significant departure from its pull for any sustained period of time. Even after life-threatening illnesses men tend to go back to workaholic and disconnected patterns and behaviors, while women continue to obsess about appearance, closeness, food, and love even in the face of tragedy.

Why have thirty years of consciousness raising via feminism and men's liberation not produced the kind of good-willed understanding that make for lasting and fulfilling relationships? The answer lies in the defensive, unconscious nature of gender process, the *how* and *why* of the masculine and feminine way of experiencing and interpreting reality.

This process is as tenacious in its compelling power as any addiction. Women can see men's defensiveness (i.e., when women tell men they are afraid to get close, are out of touch with feelings, are controlling, are never truly present, or are cold). Men encounter women's defensiveness (such as when they tell women about their tendencies to be engulfing, blaming and guilt-making, insecure, naïve, bottomless in their need for reassurance, irrational in their thought processes and emotional responses, and manipulative with their sexuality). Men can see the defensiveness in women, and vice-versa, but rarely can either gender see their own defensive overreactions, rigidities, and distortions. Thus, when relationships end, both sexes tend to see what has been done to them, but rarely what they have done to create their own failures and pain.

The lack of awareness of gender process erodes the hard work that women and men have done and continue to do to raise their consciousness. Romance tends to transform into anger, and men and women's best intentions still tend to be misconstrued by the other.

Men today pay a great price for what they still don't know about relationships and themselves. Often they can't distinguish a woman's manipulative response from real caring. Men are surprised when women construe men's attempts at humor as hostility. They are blinded by accusations of abuse, harassment, and sexual misconduct when they thought their actions were understood. Men believe they are clear only to find that women experience their "agreements" much differently. Divorce and custody battles often leave men's lives in shambles as men discover too late that their best efforts at having been responsive and good fathers and husbands were experienced much differently than what they believed.

This is a book for men about a woman's process; how to interpret, understand, and respond to it; and about his counterpart process, and how that creates his relationship prisms, blind spots, self-defeating behaviors, defensive reactions, and patterns. I believe this book can help to erase the notion that women and men are mysteries to each other or from different worlds. While women may be impossible to understand using traditional masculine logic, it is possible for men who become conscious of the nature of process, their own and the woman's, to decipher and respond to their relationships effectively and accurately. Men who try to understand their relationships with logic will be defeated and left confused.

It is not what a man does but what his process is (his personal impact) and what the woman experiences as a result, that determines the direction and emotions within his relationship. What she experiences and feels with him often have little connection to what he intends or believes his impact to be.

1 What Men Still Don't Know About Themselves

✓ The Personal Journey of Masculinity: From
Externalization to Disconnection to Oblivion

✓ Men's Relationship Enemies are Truly Within

✓ What Little Boys and Men are Made Of

✓ Men's Behavior Doesn't Make Sense Either

✓ Masculine Addition

The Personal Journey of Masculinity:
From Externalization to Disconnection to Oblivion

"I'm not sure I ever 'got it' when it comes to how to live my life in a way that was original and free," reflected Steven Salt, a retired businessman. "Of course, like most men, I always believed I had the answers and that I was not going to live my life the stupid way other men do. I was going to be unique and avoid their mistakes, but instead I'm just another male stereotype. I started off thinking that being an achiever and a 'winner' would be the key to real freedom. So all my energy went that way and I faked everything else when it came to caring about other people. Then I thought I'd marry the 'perfect' woman and be the 'perfect' dad and husband, not like the other married men. I'd be different. But no matter how I tried I was forcing it and probably fooling no one but myself. My wife finally left and I barely know who my kids really are. When we talk it's mainly 'business.' I fell into all the traps. Now that I'm in my seventies, I'm becoming just like all those guys I felt sorry for when I was younger—guys with no real friends and with no patience for anyone else's ideas or opinions. I can barely stand to talk to anyone and yet I'm still looking to fulfill myself by meeting the 'perfect' woman. I've become a macho cliché. It's taken me this long to realize that even if she existed I really wouldn't know how to be with her and make it feel good anyway."

Content is what makes one man's life seem different or better than the next man's: one man is an athlete, the other a mechanic, the third is a lawyer, and the fourth is homeless. What men still don't know is that *process* relentlessly chips away and shapes the essence of each man's life, his relationships, his habits and/or addictions, his body awareness, his preoccupations, and his relationships to his children.

The successful man who is the most admired becomes that way because his process is the extreme, and while the world applauds him, everything personal, from relationships to body awareness to sexuality and self-awareness, erodes and creates havoc with the life he lives and knows, not the life outsiders see and imagine.

The psychoanalyst and the car mechanic both hear similar things from their wives and inspire similar feelings from their children. The fact that the psychoanalyst is an expert on personality and relationships does not help him in the face of his own process. Like all men, he hears that he has an obnoxious ego, is impossible to get close to, and is controlling, cold, critical, and angry. Perhaps the psychoanalyst responds to it with loftier sounding words, but the essence of the experience, the feelings and the impact, are the same as for the automobile mechanic or the short-order cook.

Process is the great equalizer because while exaggerated masculine process may give a man an attractive outward image, in his intimate relationship with a woman it exacts the most extreme price in the form of a painful, out of control, and "crazy" marriage, plus alienation, rejection, and even antipathy from his children, along with an absence of caring friends or any real supportive network.

Masculine process has at its foundation *externalization*. The young boy is focused away from his inner and personal self and into achievement, performance, competition, success, emotional control (being "cool"), autonomy (not being dependent or needy), fearlessness, action, and an ethic that only values time spent in *doing*. Anything else is suspect and viewed as lazy, worthless, time-wasting, or meaningless.

Externalization, or the process of being pushed outside of oneself, amplifies and eventually becomes *disconnection*. Personal relationships are then objectified and founded on the role another can play in his life. Relationships are based on *doing* and are therefore fairly readily interchangeable with anyone else who can *do*.

Disconnection leads men to the experience of being loners, where it's "lonely at the top," and freedom, space, and "doing one's thing," are the rationalized values. Disconnection transforms a man into someone who has everything he wanted externally, but has nothing that is bonded or connected on a personal level. He is "out of touch," so he doesn't know why he's unhappy, and may conclude that the cause of his malaise is that he needs "more." He sets out to get it, but when he gets it he feels deader and more isolated than ever.

The end stage of this journey of masculine process is personal *oblivion*, which can occur early in his life or may not appear full blown until he's an older man, depending on how extreme his externalized process is. At this point, personal connection becomes impossible. He doesn't know he rationalizes his personal emptiness with cynical philosophies and escapes painful awareness through non-relationships he can control by buying. In the end state of oblivion, he is beyond personal reach and can only relate in abstract, depersonalized, intellectualized ways. The only way he is "loved" is in return for providing or taking care of others.

Men's Relationship Enemies are Truly Within

A man's externalization makes women and others feel pushed away, as if no bond or connection is possible with him. To understand that better, a man needs only to think back to times when he tried to be close to or make friends with another man. Even if the other man may initially have seemed to be a "great guy," responsible and seemingly friendly, no close friendship or bond developed. He finally gave up trying because it never felt like any ongoing personal connection could be created, regardless of the effort made.

A man's ego leads him to believe the unbelievable, particularly when a woman he just met seems instantly to "fall in love," and tells him how wonderful and special he is. He believes that her adoring response can actually be founded in reality.

A man's limited personal focus and capacity cause him to want any relationship he is in to be easy and effortless. So he chooses an accommodating woman who makes it easy for him because *she* wants and needs him. Without her push, the relationship falters and dies.

Men's personal disconnection creates an intense buildup of denied vulnerability, loneliness, and neediness in him. A powerful vacuum is created in him that is easily filled by a woman who is "nice" to him and knows how to push the buttons that make him feel good.

Relationships are exceedingly complex, yet romance and intense needs on the part of men and women cause them to begin quickly and feel like magical or destined events. Intimate relationships defy masculine logic and women are as impervious to men's use of cold logic as men are to an outpouring of tears and emotion.

The shambles of male/female relationships are readily seen. Many of these dramas are acted out in the public arena. These are the relationship experiences of famous, successful men who were used to being in control and who found themselves in passionate romances that exploded suddenly and spun horribly out of control. While all of these men were capable of logic and understanding, they were destructive and damaged because of massive relationship blind spots.

Blaming and guilt are hallmarks of traditional male/female relationships, while goodwill and self-awareness are usually absent. Men are endangered in relationships because society tends to lay the burden of the problems on them. They are viewed as mainly responsible for the abuse, violence, and pain that take place. When a man is accused of sexism, harassment, or abuse, his own lack of awareness, coupled with the negative interpretations of society, place him on the defensive. When he tries to explain or defend himself, often he makes matters worse.

Heterosexual men are vulnerable because they are deeply dependent on their relationships with women for personal connection and fulfillment. It is primarily here that they look for love, whereas women connect for closeness and love in many places, such as with family, friends, and children.

The bigger they come, the harder they fall. The stronger the masculine façade, the more rigid and in denial he is of his dependency, isolation, self-doubts, neediness, and vulnerability. A man's ego blocks him from seeing the deterioration of his relationships. He doesn't believe he will be left, so he can't see it coming. When it does occur, he is in shock and desperate, and he is engulfed by his blocked and denied needs and feelings.

Men see fragility in women that really characterizes men and they tend to be naïvely literal in their belief that a woman is nice. They are unable to see the anger and negative feelings building up behind the mask. Men spend their lives in the belief that they are working for their families and that *that* expresses their love, only to discover the family's interpretation of them is quite different.

Most men would be shocked if they could see themselves objectively and floored if they could see the chasm between who they think they are and the way that they are perceived by others. While they may choose to believe that they've been let down and disappointed by the people in their lives and by life itself, they have unknowingly brought everything onto themselves.

While busy "being a man," they instead became slaves to their illusions and images of themselves as they moved progressively into their own world of "being right," "being better," "being untouchable," and "being free." Turns out that they were none of those things.

To move away from being their own worst enemies and creating their own illusions and disappointments, they will need to first recognize how they processed the realities of their lives and the way their process created the predictable nightmares of their experience. There's no real mystery to it, only each man's inability, fear, and resistance to seeing the *how* of their lives, rather than the *what*—the *way they were* versus the symbols they used to define and explain themselves.

What Little Boys and Men are Made of

When we experience a male as acting like "a real man," we are unknowingly responding to the full impact of separate embedded process components or defenses operating within him. Specifically, how he expresses or blocks needs and emotions such as fear and dependency on others defines him as a man. While the overt package may make him seem outwardly very attractive, that attractiveness is composed of defensive elements that will create inevitable endpoints in his relationships and in his life.

Thomas had the outward appearance of a "real man," the "perfect man." From the time he was young, he was told that he was "a winner," a guy who "had it all" and therefore could accomplish anything that he set his mind to.

Now, at age 46, he wondered what had happened to those prophecies of greatness. While as a businessman with a MBA from Pepperdine University in California, he had done well financially and had become a CEO of an export/import company. Everything else in his life had gone sour. A success in the eyes of others, he felt like a failure. Two marriages had ended badly, and his relationship to his two sons—who were on their own and rarely spoke to him—was a superficial one at best. Thomas felt lonely much of the time and physically he felt drained. With time he felt a cloud of depression floating over his head.

The story of Thomas is the story of most men who looked like winners growing up because they epitomized the ultimate in masculinity. The problems they experienced were the result of how they were as people, not *what* they were as men. *What* they were shone in the competitive world. *How* they were had to do with the way they related personally, the way that they experienced the world, the way that they expressed or didn't express their emotions and the way that they connected to family, friends, and new acquaintances.

Like many men, the way Thomas's life evolved was beyond his conscious control. His socialization as a man produced certain inevitable endpoints that were the direct result of process, the defenses that he couldn't see because they were an expression of what he was and how he felt he needed to be as a man. The components of traditional masculinity such as Thomas's are as follows:

Denied Dependency/Defensive Autonomy: A man's obsession with space, control, and distance are disguised forms of denying his dependency and defending his autonomy.

- Strength comes from not needing anyone.
- Dependency is experienced as weakness and as dangerous. Counting on others is vulnerability to be avoided.

- He is impossible to get close to but in denial of it.
- He can't ask for help.
- When he's hurting, he pulls deeper inside of himself rather than reach out and expose vulnerability.
- He is unknown to others on a personal level.
- The natural state of the "real man" is as a disconnected loner.
- As he gets older, his walls against personal connection get thicker.
- He is excessively and dangerously dependent on his partner but in denial of it until she leaves him. Then he cracks and "the bigger they come, the harder they fall."
- When he's "in danger" of getting close and dependent, he becomes distant and hostile instead.
- His humor and conversation are impersonal or distancing.
- Under stress he isolates himself. Going off alone refreshes him.
- He cannot form a permanent personal bond with another person in the absence of a goal or purpose.
- He gets his dependency needs met by taking care of others.
- His ways of distancing include intellectualizing, silence, withdrawal, and the closing off of personal interaction.
- His worldview or philosophy puts great emphasis on freedom, separateness, and independence.

Denied Fear / Defensive Aggression: Men pride themselves on never being scared, yet unknowingly cover it up by always being angry. Defensive aggression can take direct physical forms (violence), intellectualized forms (lawyering: "my ideas are the right ones," "I'm right, you're wrong"), psychological and emotional forms (insensitivity, coldness, hostility, belittling), or social forms (competitiveness, empire building).

- When feeling vulnerable, he responds aggressively.
- Acknowledgment or giving in to fear is experienced

as weakness. He loses connection to the basic survival instinct of fear and sometimes is destroyed by denying it.

- Aggression projected creates a worldview for him that "life is a jungle," and creates in him a paranoid posture in the world that may be disguised by surface "niceness," compulsive politeness, and addiction to work.
- His worldview stresses power, strength, "might makes right," and only the strong survive and thrive.
- His life orientation involves preparing for and protecting himself against the world and the future. He builds fortresses of power and control and isolates himself in the process.
- He doesn't really trust anybody.
- Potential "macho-psychotic" behaviors include explosive, inappropriate fighting over senseless issues, fighting to prove he's not afraid, and accepting meaningless yet life-threatening challenges.
- He creates a cynical, power-based, distrustful philosophy of life.
- His is a bottomless well of competitiveness and self-protection.
- He transforms play into a tension-filled war (e.g., tennis matches where every shot is a bullet), and he becomes self-loathing when he loses.

Blocked Submission/Defensive Need to Control: Never giving in is a man's strength. Giving up control is seen as weakness.

- His philosophy is "My way or no way."
- He denies his controlling personality, but others shy away and avoid involvement with him due to its impact.
- "Macho-psychotic" potential is embedded in his resistance to submission. He will risk his life to prove "No one tells me what to do, and no one pushes me around."
- The highest compliment to his mind is, "He's in complete control."

- Interpersonal control is seen via his inability to take in the ideas of others and how easily he gets bored when listening to other people, even if he hides that fact behind a veneer of being nice.
- When he participates in something he hasn't chosen, he is unhappy and bored.
- He pulls away from everything and everybody that he can't control.

Blocked Emotion / Defensive Intellectualization: Men hide the emotional, inflate the rational, and barricade themselves from the vulnerable.

- He is cold and personally detached.
- He can't truly empathize with the feelings or internal experiences of others.
- He distrusts emotions and emotional displays.
- He turns personal problems in relationships into intellectual discussions that involve logical problem solving.
- He is vulnerable to psychosomatic illnesses from repressed emotions.
- His inner deadness creates the need for intense outer stimulation. On a personal level, he is easily bored. He craves external distraction and excitement in order to feel fully alive.
- Emotional displays by others make him uncomfortable and may be viewed as irrational, indications of weakness, or as craziness.
- He develops elaborate philosophies of life to explain how things really are. However, he can't see his own process and how it creates the personal reality he experiences, which he then creates life philosophies to rationalize.
- He lives by so-called objective truths that are neither objective nor true.
- He has an exaggerated respect for and belief in the power of the intellect to change life experience.

- He can't understand intimate relationships (i.e., his children, his wife and friends) when these relationships become dysfunctional.
- He is easily manipulated on a personal level by accommodation and ego strokes because he can't distinguish real emotions from fake ones. His ego craves flattering messages.
- He applauds the intellect and the scientific and he has contempt or distrust for emotion and intuition.

Blocked Sensuality/Intimacy and Defensive Sexuality: A man's sexuality can be understood as sexual excitement without closeness.

- He gets closeness and dependency needs met through sex. Therefore, sex becomes a compulsive drive.
- He objectifies his need for women and closeness by sexualizing them.
- His sexuality is cold, detached, and disconnected from personal feeling, though it may be disguised as personal.
- He withdraws, falls asleep, or otherwise cuts off and disconnects once he is sexually sated.
- There is a buildup of painful tension if he is sexually deprived.
- He is uncomfortable with affectionate touching and non-sexually motivated physical intimacy.
- When he can't perform sexually, he loses his outlet for physical intimacy and tension builds. That is a main reason why dysfunction causes him great anxiety.

Blocked Internalization and Personal Connection/Defensive Externalization and Disconnection: A man distracts himself by always *doing* in order to escape from his discomfort with simply feeling, or *being.*

- Personal experiences are perceived and related to impersonally or abstractly and are not really experienced or felt in the moment, thus cutting him off from his inner self.

- His focus is on doing and on activity as his way of relating.
- He requires high levels of external stimulation and distraction in order to feel alive.
- He interprets sex, health, and relationships in impersonal, disconnected ways. The body is experienced and viewed as a machine made up of disconnected parts; sexually, the penis is experienced as disconnected plumbing and people are objects to be related to mechanically.
- His personal relationships are with objects or abstractions, such as his automobile, possessions, money, or the pursuit of "truth."
- He cannot create a true and lasting personal connection or relationship.
- He ends his life in personal isolation, and others close to him may even be secretly relieved by his death.

Blocked "In The Moment" Relating/Defensive Goal Orientation: A man's persistent focus on attaining a goal allows him an escape from personal relating.

- Personally, he is never fully present and therefore is easily distracted when in personal interaction.
- Meanings are given to goal-oriented activities, and an activity without a goal or purpose is meaningless.

The Predictable Projected Reality Created by Masculine Process

The sum total of all these blocked and exaggerated parts of a man create a certain predictable and narrow reality that men believe is objectively true when, in fact, it is composed of a series of twisted endpoints that propel their lives in a way that make isolation, deadness, personal alienation, and rigidity the hallmarks of their existence.

The irony for Thomas, as for all men raised like he had been, believing they were masters of their environment, was that the opposite was true. What men still don't know is that they are the pawns of the process that is a result of their so-called manliness.

Men's Behavior Doesn't Make Sense Either

Men find women hard to understand because they approach and analyze them as they would a mechanical problem—externally and based on the observable information. Focused in that way, much of what goes on with women doesn't make sense to men. Men only see inconsistencies, contradictions, and irrationalities.

To understand women, men need to understand their *process*, specifically, the way that women experience reality. The distortions in women's perceptions are the complementary opposite to the distortions in men's perceptions. The issue isn't just that women experience reality differently, but that they experience it in a polarized or opposite way. In their outlook on life, for example, most men see a competitive jungle and believe it is dangerous to be vulnerable, dependent, or indecisive, while most women tend to see love as a guiding principle and consider people as a whole to be "nice," with openness and vulnerability as a path to personal connection and fulfillment.

Women use the word "nice" the way men use the word "bullshit." Men tend to be cynical, while women tend to be Pollyannaish. So men pursue power and distance while women pursue love and connection.

Logically, men's relationship behaviors seem as crazy and inexplicable to women as women's behaviors appear to men. Men understand what they do, but to women, men's behavior is as irrational as the hysterical screaming of a woman is to a man. To the woman, it is unfathomable that a man:

- with an attractive, loving wife would pursue other women, even prostitutes, for sex.
- would want to have sex, a physically intimate act, with a woman he has just met, or is not close to emotionally.
- will leave a caring wife and children to pursue a young

woman he's obviously enthralled with for the superficial reason that she is young, sexually attractive, available, and accommodating.

- will discontinue a good relationship with a woman he's dating and not tell her why.
- who is "always" working to provide for his family barely makes an effort to spend involved personal time with them.
- who can't relate to his wife and his own children is busy fighting causes, developing theories and philosophies, and defending principles to change the world.
- would rather be right than close and loving, will alienate people to prove that he is correct, and will turn a simple request for a hug or a conversation into grounds for a verbal discussion.
- who has the "good life" would be so untrusting and cynical.
- will play sports or games with his friends or children, and transform a fun activity into a mini-war of competition, replete with expletives, temper flare-ups, and self-hating comments if he loses.

Men need to know that irrational behavior is in the eye of the beholder!

Masculine Addiction

Women see it when they say that men can't love or relate. Children see it when they close up around their fathers and never share anything personal with them. Men see it in other men, when they avoid or don't bother to attempt anything personal with each other. Beneath men's many addictions, one process underlies them all: the defensive process I term *masculine addiction*.

Masculine addiction, which develops as a way of escaping the inner self of personal needs, vulnerable emotion, gender identity confusion, and other threats to the masculine image, destroys men's personal relationship connection capacity. It does this by sealing the inner self off from awareness and replacing it with a focus on the impersonal, and creating a mechanical way of relating.

The tension and frustration produced by the blocked-off inner self is contained and controlled by a variety of addictions that provide temporary relief, and are mechanical and disconnected. Everything from life problems, to women, to one's own children and one's health and sexuality are experienced in an externalized, disconnected way. Masculine process prevents men from seeing how they filter their lives through a series of defensive and externalized responses.

The masculine addictions replace the inner, personal capacity for relating and experiencing. The external focus provides channels for achieving, relating, and experiencing pleasure while systematically walling off and destroying the inner personal self.

Men deny their addictions or make light of them when confronted by others (i.e., "You're always watching sports," "You sexualize everything," or "Don't you think about anything except work and making money?"). They are seemingly all part of "being a man." Like all addictions, however, they destroy the personal as they provide temporary pleasure, distraction, and escape from inner conflicts and fears.

Initially, these addictions give a man the sensation of being manly. The more intense the denied inner conflict, needs, impulses and emotional vulnerability, the more intense the addictions to externalization outlets needed to contain them. In some ways, it works temporarily; in other ways, it creates long-term tragedy. An 18-year-old male may be a genius at taking apart Porsche motors because he literally can identify with that machine, but he stays stoned in the meantime, and his personal life is a shambles. The Porsche motor work gives him a channel, while the drugs and booze give him relief and escape from his repressed inner self. Combined, they destroy his relationship capacity and self.

Like all addictions, the initial experiences of masculine addiction, which involves forms of cutting off the internal experience and fusing with the external, are exciting. However, an increasing personal deadening process begins. Soon, a maintenance dose is necessary just to keep away the anxiety and depression that follow the crippling of the personal self.

Masculine addiction, which numbs and deadens the inner, personal, vulnerable self and creates a façade of cool and invulnerable strength, produces a concomitant need and craving for external stimulation, external excitement, and escape from inner personal tension caused by loneliness. When pulled into a personal encounter that may trigger threatening feelings and conflicts, masculine addiction kicks in and the personal is replaced by the need to have a drink, turn on the TV, go off alone, be sexual, work, work out, or get stoned. All are there to help him escape from the buildup of inner tension.

Like all addictions, masculine addiction is denied and unfelt, so men cannot see themselves escaping from their inner selves. To the contrary, men believe they relate personally. They compartmentalize and see their addictions as only a way of doing things that "feel good," and are perceived as healthy, manly pursuits.

Denial of a man's masculine addictions remains at least until after tremendous personal damage has been done and his personal life is a shambles. Even then, acknowledgment of the various forms of his addictive behaviors designed to disconnect himself will be avoided, the disasters blamed on something else, and quick external solutions sought.

Because masculine addiction has not really been identified or recognized for what it is and how it comes to be, its damaging byproducts, such as a man's dysfunctional family relationships, are blamed instead on alcoholism, womanizing, violent outbursts, mood swings, or compulsive working. But all come from the same defensive process.

Men have many ways of rationalizing this. Finally, they may decide it's best just to be left alone in order to engage in their addictions. Then there is burnout, despair, and self-destruction because they come to see no way out of the self-created nightmare of these bottomless addictions that leave them painfully isolated.

How much is enough money, sex, power, control, autonomy, "deepest truth," or other addictive pursuits, and what are these doing to men? When annihilation of the personal self is complete, desperation and frustration may become overwhelming.

As a therapist, I have noticed that change is hardest and slowest for men most addicted to socially applauded pursuits such as success, money, and power. The personal self has the greatest amount of anxiety and terror underneath, which explains why these men are externally focused, rigid, and closed off on the surface.

When everything personal has been severely damaged, byproduct addictions intensify. Men work harder, drink more, accumulate more money, or pursue more meaningless sex. This may allow them to have the sense of a simulated personal self.

I was therapist to a wealthy 72-year-old man with an explosive temper. His first wife had committed suicide. He had three other dysfunctional marriages and four troubled children, one of whom had died of AIDS. His fourth marriage, to a woman 30 years younger, was filled with conflict and boredom. Still, he was rigidly addicted to working and making money. He experienced near panic when either his work was interfered with or money was not made. He distrusted the world, got close to nobody, and money became his misguided protection. His wealth and success prolonged his denial about the effect of his masculine addiction and disconnected process. The addiction to work and money gave him a sense of relief, pleasure, and safety.

While we may celebrate the so-called positive addictions and righteously moralize about the negative ones, the ultimate impact of all of them, if they are expressions of masculine addiction, is similar, and the extent of personal damage depends not on the particular habits involved, but on the degree of personal disconnection and externalization that become his process. They destroy the inner self and lead a man to personal oblivion.

Masculine addiction begins with mainly an upside, or a "feel good." The damage created is rarely visible in the beginning. In fact, the addiction is often encouraged by those who would rather see a man "die as a man" than become a vulnerable and possibly unsuccessful "non-manly" person. Young men are often reckless in their attempts to have a good time because just *being*, in a personal way, creates too much anxiety and discomfort. We ritualize and sanctify the early stages of the destruction of the personal male self. We make light of getting drunk and "getting laid" as time-honored masculine rituals.

What is being celebrated in these masculine rituals are the first obvious signs of the loss of the personal and connected self, along with the beginnings of serious body, brain, and nerve damage. Like all addictions, masculine addiction initially feels great because it reassures the man, and everyone else, that he is normal.

Some men eventually come to see their masculine addiction, usually only after everything personal has been destroyed or severely damaged; others never become aware of it. They float off into a personal oblivion, perhaps propped up by a long-suffering wife and by the comfort of their escape rituals until they die, having passed the damage on to the next generations.

My 72-year-old client yelled at his wife for shopping too much and for being careless with money. He could see her addictions, but he denied his own. At age 72, he was more obsessed about money than he was at age 50 when he had much longer to live and more reason to be a workaholic.

In masculine addiction, part of a man knows that he is addicted and that his compulsive pursuits and behaviors don't make sense— behaviors like cursing himself when he's made a bad shot in tennis, or becoming panicked because he can't get an erection, or feeling irritated and staying glued to the TV when someone personal in his life wants to talk to him. However, when he tries to change, the tensions and conflict that build within him cause him to go back to the addictive behaviors.

The signs of masculine addiction include:

- Feelings of relief and relaxation when he can close himself off from personal involvement. In other words, he is refreshed by isolation or other forms of personal withdrawal.
- Avoidance of any social engagements unless they have a purpose or he *has* to attend. He doesn't actively seek them out.
- The telephone rarely or never rings with personal

phone calls. With each passing year, these phone calls are fewer and shorter in duration, if there are any.

- When watching television or doing an activity, his initial spontaneous reaction when someone talks to him is irritation and annoyance.
- He believes that abstract Truth is a noble pursuit that can set him and others free and make life better. He believes that truth, logic, and answers are the highest goods and he wants to pursue and uncover them in order to create the good life.
- He goes for days without physical, affectionate, non-sexual touching or intimate conversation and he doesn't notice or miss them.
- He's into exercising and workouts, which tend to get longer and more regular. He feels a great sense of accomplishment over that and continually tries to increase performance standards.
- Money is increasingly important, no matter how much he has. When he adds to his pile, he feels good, though it never quells his thirst for more. What he does have never seems quite enough. More money gives him a sense of safety, but the feeling doesn't last long. Losing money upsets or petrifies him.
- His idea of a great relationship is the latest partner, while the relationships of his past seem like negative distant memories.
- Winning, being right, and achieving are the major goals of his life although the satisfaction he gets from them progressively decreases.
- When at home, his idea of relaxing is essentially being left alone to read the paper, watch the news, have a drink, and go over the mail.
- He may believe that he likes his partner, but he wishes she would talk less.
- During personal conversations, his mind wanders, he gets distracted or bored, and he can't concentrate.

- Being touched or hugged unexpectedly is disconcerting and uncomfortable.
- His "best friends" don't live near him, and he rarely sees them.

Masculine addiction is harmful and costly, no matter what the short-term rewards are. It produces rigidity, defensiveness, overreaction, poor personal judgment, burnout, isolation, and paranoia, and it incurs the resentment of others. Because it destroys his personal relationship capacity, it ultimately negates the pleasures of his external accomplishments. No one else really cares about them.

Those who promote masculine addiction as part of the experience and glory of being a man are cheerleaders for men's denial of the destruction of a man's personal self. They are pandering to the man who would like to avoid the anxiety and turbulence involved in reconnecting with his inner, personal self.

Masculinity as an Addiction: Its Composition

- Masculine compulsions to perform, achieve, and succeed are bottomless.
- It requires more and more to simply maintain his sense of being successful.
- His judgment is impaired in the pursuit of his gratifications. He does self-defeating things.
- With an absence of gratification and stimulation, his anxiety and desperation build rapidly toward an "I've got to have it" experience.
- Proving himself is more important than caring for himself. He'd rather "die like a man" than live otherwise.
- The irrational motivations of driven, out-of-control masculinity, such as success, power, autonomy, wealth, and control, are impervious to logical restraint or rational control.
- When he's young, the gratification of proving himself excites and validates him. As he gets older, gratification

is compulsively sought to protect himself against encroaching self-doubt, self-hate, and the fear of being nobody.

- There is no learning: His self-destructive compulsions are repeated endlessly, even as the price for them increases.
- The craving is always for "more." There is never enough. The bar is raised continually and past successes are no consolation.
- Other people are objects to be used in the pursuit of his gratification.
- There is never enough success, power, wealth, autonomy, control, or sexuality.
- There is growing distrust of others and isolation as the pace of his pursuits accelerates. Everybody in the way is pushed aside.
- His ever-expanding ego makes it impossible to hear others, even as he believes that he *is* really listening. In personal conversation, there is increasing distractibility, boredom, and an inability to concentrate. As his attention span decreases, his need for intense stimulation in order to focus outside of himself increases.
- Increasing inner numbness, deadness, emptiness, and a craving for excitement in order to feel alive grow as he gets older.
- The inevitable endpoints of his defensive process are isolation, disappointment, and a giving up of efforts to alter his course, until the final crash.

Ultimately, all addictions are the same. What distinguishes one from the other is only that some are visible and socially unacceptable, whereas others fall into cultural blind spots and get applauded. The latter are the addictions society seems to need in order to keep the system and economy going. Nevertheless, the essence of all addictions is a form of self-destruction, even if society chooses to deny that and even thrives on the products of the addiction. The bottomless cravings, the distorted perceptions, the faulty judgments, the denial, and the manipulation and exploitation required to feed it are as true for masculine addiction as they are for addiction to drugs or alcohol. While changing the addictive patterns may initially seem overwhelming and even impossible, in fact it is a journey in which every step away from the cravings leads to a healthier, more fluid way of being.

2 What Men Still Don't Know About Women

✓ "A Woman" is an Abstraction

✓ The Content/Process Paradox

✓ Where a Woman's "Distortions" Come From

✓ Reactors are "Nice," Dangerous, and "Impossible" to Understand

✓ Is She Really "In Touch?"

✓ The Problem with Traditional Women

✓ A Blamer is a Blamer is a Blamer

✓ Relating to a Woman: The Best and the Worst of it

✓ Why Men Withdraw and Become Silent in Intimate Relationships

✓ The Problem with a Woman's Low Self-Esteem

✓ The Very Spiritual Woman

✓ Eating Addictions: Food is Feminine Booze

✓ Men Wonder Why: Common and Not-So-Common Questions Men Ask about Women

"A Woman" Is an Abstraction

Ronald, an engineer and a bachelor at age 31, felt a deep longing and loneliness that he believed would be assuaged and healed if he could only find the right woman. He did everything he knew to do to make that happen. He asked friends to fix him up, joined all manner of groups where single women might show, and cruised Internet dating sites.

In spite of his intense fantasy about the "special woman," and his very logical way of meeting and solving life's problem, he kept forgetting that he had already felt sure he had met her many times in the past. In ten years of very active dating, he had met and dated at least 200 women. Many excited him initially and made him believe and feel that she might be the one. Once the initial excitement faded, however, and it came time to deal with the reality of being in a relationship, he would get discouraged and disillusioned. There always seemed to be something wrong. Sometimes, he blamed his own deficiencies. Other times he recognized a major flaw in the woman. More experiences only increased his confusion and wariness. While he believed he should be gaining in his knowledge and understanding of relationships, time passing only caused him to feel more hopeless and confused. Yet, he continued his search for *the* woman, or even just *a* woman to spend time with.

A Woman's Process Creates a Man's Experience

"A woman" is an abstraction that conjures up fantasies of closeness, sex, love, meaning in life, special friendship, fun, emotional support, understanding, and sensual pleasures. These are a few of the components of the fantasy as the hope and dream generated by "man meets woman" begins.

The fantasy is bolstered by the physical: Her face, clothes, hair, smile, body, smell, and feminine style all add to the initial excitement he feels. A woman's process, or how it is to be with her based on her conditioning and socialization from the time she was a little girl, however, creates a man's experience with her. Her upbringing has created her needs, the way she reacts and interprets encounters and events, the things that frighten her, and the way she relates to men. That process shapes, tears at, transforms, and finally dissolves the initial fantasy, and creates the actual experience that a man will have.

Someone to be Close To

A man's initial fantasy about a woman is as someone to be close to. His actual experience, however, will be determined by her process—specifically, by the intensity of her needs for attention and commitment and how quickly and strongly these emerge. Furthermore, the longer her needs are juxtaposed against a man's need to be separate and free, the more she will transform from a pleasing fantasy into a major stressor and irritation. "Someone to be close to" then becomes an onerous burden, rather than a fulfillment of his dreams.

Someone to Enjoy Sex With

A man's initial fantasy about a woman may be as someone to have great sex with. The reality of that will be generated by the way she experiences and reacts to sex. What men still don't know is that due to her socialization, sex for her is only occasionally an act of physical lust, excitement, and pleasure. Rather, it is a way to create closeness, to gain control and power, to move toward commitment, to be held, and to get affection. The actual act of intercourse is a low priority, and rarely anything like what men fantasize sex with her will be like.

Where a man initially thought that what he really wanted was to have sex with a woman, after sex he may find himself compartmentalizing. He would like to get the good stuff while avoiding the negatives and he will find that it can't be done. If he continues to try to get it his way, he will confront her disappointment, anger, and withdrawal, or maybe even her desperation and "crazy" demands.

Someone Who will Really Understand Me

The fantasy a man has when he meets a woman, that she will be "someone to talk to who will really understand me," also is radically transformed by the reality created by her feminine process. The desire to have someone to talk to will be thwarted and eroded by the fact that often she experiences his verbal communications differently than he intends them. More often than not, she reacts to his conversation but doesn't initiate any conversation of interest to him. His efforts at freely and openly communicating himself to her may even be experienced negatively. He is bewildered as the misunderstandings during conversation increase, and she perceives him as angry, insensitive, self-centered, critical, distant, cynical, and cold. His humor or attempts at being funny may be perceived by her as crude, or even as hostile and hurtful.

The fantasy of having "someone to talk to who will really understand me" will dissolve. In its place will arise difficulty in finding anything at all to say that is safe, so eventually he talks less. As he does that, her negative reactions increase and "someone to talk to who understands" becomes something that's far worse than having nobody to talk to. She wants communication and connection, but there is precious little safe and mutual ground to make that a reality.

A Companion to Have Fun With

The initial fantasy about her as "a companion to have fun with" also is transformed. Her process will create the reality. If she *reacts* to his ideas of what to do, rather than initiates or acts, he will continually have to generate activities of interest to her and that will be hard to do. Then he may hear her assertions that he is controlling, or he will feel guilty when he chooses wrong. "Having fun" will be reduced to eating, shopping, or going to the movies.. These may be alien to his sense of what having fun is, so having fun erodes and he finds himself bored and withdrawn, and blamed for that also.

Once a man begins to look at the how of his experiences with women (i.e., how they related to him, how they responded to conflict, how they interpreted his humor and directness), relationships can then become more real and less random.

The Content/Process Paradox

What men still don't know is that content is what makes potential relationships seem like they should be easy, fun, and satisfying. Polarized gender process is why relationships turn out to be stressful, tangled webs of miscommunication, and produce a sense of discomfort and anxiety. Real relationships are rarely fun or easy between a man and a woman once their processes combine and push the attractive content into the background. Expecting that they should be fun and enjoyable will create feelings of failure and inadequacy in the man because he believes that he is responsible for the failure to meet those expectations.

Being aware of process, his and hers, provides a map for growth and reality. Working on transforming process is the challenge. With effort, a proper fit, endurance, and self-awareness, relationships can become fulfilling. When stuck at the level of abstraction and fantasy ("I need a woman"), disappointment, disillusionment, or worse becomes the reality.

A Traditional Woman's Process: Its Components and the Reality it Creates in Relationships

A woman's process is internalized. Typically, the vulnerable or inner self is defensively exaggerated while her overt power side is suppressed. The following are feminine process components that will shape her relationship responses and behaviors. When something is referred to as repressed, it means that it is blocked and not a part of her conscious awareness and response repertoire.

Repressed Aggression/Defensive Fear: In the pursuit of pure romance, a woman loses touch with her anger, while her fears are amplified.

- She represses and denies her own anger.
- She overreacts and exaggerates a man's anger and

aggression, and sees it as more than it is; she tells him, "You're always angry," or "You scare me." He doesn't understand why.

- She experiences herself as the victim when problems arise.
- She expresses her anger passively and indirectly and in non-negotiable ways, such as by procrastinating and chronically being late.
- She avoids difficult issues and withdraws in the face of conflict and confrontation, even over seemingly minor issues.
- She takes the moral high road by seeing herself as the loving and giving one and her partner as the love spoiler.
- She is afraid for no apparent reason.
- She cries when she is angry.
- She yearns for and strives to create an all-loving, conflict-free relationship that is impossible to achieve and will cause disappointment and bitterness in her.
- She imagines that the relationship would work if he would only try harder to be nice.
- She believes that continually "being nice" is possible.

Repressed Autonomy/Defensive Craving for Closeness: In romance, a woman strives to make two become as one.
- She seeks an ever-increasing fusion or closeness.
- She complains of a lack of intimacy.
- She desires continual reassurance that she is loved.
- She sees her partner as fearful of closeness if he resists her need for more close contact.
- She reacts with anxiety and distress to distance and separation.
- She implies that he is willfully hurtful and rejecting for wanting to do things on his own.
- She comes to the conclusion that she can't get her deeper needs for love met with him.
- She loses her sense of self and identity in the

relationship, and blames him for the loss.

Repressed Assertion/Defensive Accommodation: In the desire to please, a woman loses touch with her own separate goals and desires.

- She resists making decisions or clearly indicating what she does or does not want.
- She avoids initiating activities and instead primarily reacts to his choices.
- She appears to be happy with his choices and decisions while denying her real feelings and reactions.
- She loses her boundaries and her ability to say no.
- She allows herself to be controlled by him and then feels angry about it.
- She has low self-esteem; she believes that he is not interested in what she wants or has to say and that he doesn't value her opinion.
- She believes that she is being abused and taken advantage of.
- She feels that she has lost her identity because of him.
- She becomes convinced that he is uninterested in what she has to say.
- She expects him to read her mind or figure out what she wants and then feels hurt and resentful when he fails to do so.

Repressed Sexuality/Defensive Sensuality: Women develop a resistance to non-committed sexuality along with an exaggerated desire for affectionate sensuality. Men struggle as they see a woman's hot sexuality disappear, replaced by her growing desire for hugs and kisses.

- She turns her sexuality on or off depending on how she is feeling toward him.
- She believes she is being used for sex because he wants it and she can do without it.

- She gives confusing and conflicting messages as to whether or not she really wants sex.
- She uses her sexuality as a vehicle for control and power.
- She desires and prefers non-sexual forms of intimacy.
- She accuses him of not being affectionate and of primarily wanting sex.

Repressed Objectivity/Defensive Emotionality: As feelings take over, facts and information lose their relevance. This process factor creates reactions in her that are subjective and emotionally based.

- She becomes irrational under stress—such as during an argument—and says things that don't make sense to him.
- She experiences her partner as cold and insensitive when he tries to talk about their problems and differences logically or "reasonably."
- She interprets reality based on her emotional response to it. That is, if she feels something to be true then it must be real, regardless of its basis in fact.
- She is attracted to the mystical, magical, and spiritual.
- She responds based on non-logical intuition and makes emotionally based decisions.
- She perceives his objective conversations about the relationship as cold and unloving.

Repressed Goal Focus/Defensive Involvement with the Present: The future gets lost and present concerns are all that seem to count.

- She is overly tied to the present.
- She resists and denies longer-range considerations in her decisions, responses, and planning.
- She thinks in terms of "always" and "never" when she is frustrated because she is immersed in the present.
- She gets overly caught up in the moment and is unable to get going or to move on. She has trouble ending personal conversations and telephone calls or saying goodbye

- She is frequently late, procrastinates, and becomes overwhelmed by pressure from him to hurry.
- She perceives him as not really ever wanting to be with her.

Repressed Externalization/Defensive Internalization: A woman's feelings and relationships become her world, while what's going on "out there" becomes secondary.

- She responds personally to things that are not meant personally.
- She longs for and falls in love with a man who can take care of external matters for her and rescue her from the distress she experiences from the competitive world of power and money.
- She is preoccupied with and makes personal relationships and feelings her top priorities.
- She resists aggressive, competitive, detached endeavors and pursuits and expects him to take responsibility for them.
- She perceives a man as causing her to be frustrated and angry because of his lack of personal or intimate focus, though he is attractive to her precisely to the extent that he can rescue her from the pressure of the "real world."
- She has little genuine and objective interest in external concerns such as business or politics.
- She undermines her own external, worldly, and career ambitions and pursuits.

The Key to Understanding Her Process

In general, to understand how a woman experiences reality, a man need only flip his own habitual responses to their opposites.

She overreacts to negatives (anger, hurt, and neglect) just as he overreacts to positives (overt displays of affection such as kisses, hugs, and saying "I love you"). She is as uninterested and bored by his abstractions as he is in love with them. Similarly, he is uninterested in emotion-charged drama that enraptures her. She pursues closeness just as he seeks freedom and distance. She is as likely to use the word "nice" as he is to use the word "bullshit." She is as unfocused and preoccupied with the future as he is obsessed with it.

What men react to strongly, women tend not to be much affected by, and vice versa. Projection in a man-woman relationship, or the fantasy that someone you love or who loves you will experience reality as you do, and the denial of the polarized difference between a woman and a man, is the key element that makes women seem to men to be impossible to understand, just as it causes women to believe that men are deliberately frustrating them. Women frustrate and infuriate men to the extent that they experience things opposite to them.

Where a Woman's "Distortions" Come From

Growing up, Ronald would hear all the clichés from his father about women being mysterious, a puzzle that no man can figure out, victims of their hormones, and unpredictable or even crazy. What bothered him the most however, was the cynical notion that the female sex could not be trusted. He didn't believe it until he married a woman he met in graduate school. "One of the qualities I loved about her was that she always seemed so logical, so reasonable and easy to talk to," he would say. Periodically, however, even during their courtship, she would confront him in ways that "didn't make sense," or seemed outrageous.

She would say things such as "You scare me sometimes. You seem so angry," "You talk to me like I was a child," "You're so controlling," and the one that always bothered him the most, "I don't feel I can really trust you." He would think to himself, "Who is she talking about?"

The phenomenon of process projection is one of the elements that make men believe women are irrational, that it is hopeless to try and communicate, and that real closeness with a woman is dangerous or impossible.

To understand this phenomenon so common in male-female relationships, it is necessary to understand the undertow that accompanies a woman's process. In becoming the "nice," "sweet," "easy to get along with," and caring person, certain parts of her personality and expressiveness are blocked and disowned. This results in distorted and exaggerated perceptions and responses that are a product of seeing in her partner what she has denied in herself. This may contribute to creating self-fulfilling prophecies. Her accusations about his lack of closeness or his coldness may help to produce the very same responses that distress her.

When a man hears assertions and accusations from a woman that "don't make sense," where do they come from? Their source is her process.

- The anger she blocks and denies in herself, she sees coming at her. That causes her to overreact to and misinterpret relatively innocuous statements he makes, and see them as hostile and abusive.
- The autonomy and separateness she blocks and denies in herself, she will see coming at her. They cause her to overreact to and misinterpret separations and distance and to build them up into abandonment, rejections, and proof that he is not interested and that his love is waning.
- The assertiveness and direct taking of control that she represses and denies in herself, she sees coming at her. They cause her to overreact to and misinterpret his decisions as a desire to control her, deprive her of her identity, discount her, tell her what to do, and treat her as a child.
- The sexuality she represses and denies in herself, she sees coming at her. It causes her to overreact and misinterpret his sexual interest as pressuring and all-encompassing.
- The goal focus and long-range planning that she represses and denies in herself, causes her to interpret

his as meaning that he can never enjoy himself in the present, is always worrying about the future, and is never really "present" with her.

- The detached objectivity that she blocks in herself causes her to overreact to and interpret his attempts to be reasonable or logical as coldness and as evidence of a lack of emotional involvement and caring.

Projections are defensive and non-negotiable. Trying to prove to her that what she believes is not real is impossible. It is her reality of the relationship—the motor that guides her actions and determines her feelings. Engaging her in a debate about whether she is correct only confirms her beliefs.

Reactors are "Nice," Dangerous, and "Impossible" to Understand

There is a prevailing notion that male-female relationships have changed significantly and fundamentally in the last 40 years. Not only is this belief wrong, it is dangerously misleading. The actor/reactor dynamic, which characterizes the majority of romantic, intimate male-female interactions, is as entrenched as ever and is at the heart of the dysfunctional, painful experience of relationships. Intimate relationships between men and women are founded and maintained on this dynamic. Women's rage toward men, as well as men's guilt in relationships, is in direct proportion to the degree to which it is present.

In highly traditional relationships, in which men and women behave in classically traditional ways, the course of the relationship from romance to boredom and chronic tension to endpoints of rage in the woman and guilt, self-hatred, and a feeling of futility in the man are standard and predictable. No couple escapes these endpoints, though they may vary in the way they manifest them. In pure, undiluted form, the woman feels the rage directly and says, "I feel controlled. I feel I have no identity. He treats me like a child, and my self-esteem is very low. I'm frustrated and depressed."

In its indirect form, specifically with women whose belief

systems forbid them from leaving or rebelling or where fear of being on her own is extreme, the rage might be expressed as an endless series of physical complaints, health problems, fatigue, total lack of interest in sex, extreme religiosity, devotion to a guru or therapist, and an ongoing sense of being on the verge of a nervous breakdown or of depression.

The man in this traditional dance feels ongoing guilt and inadequacy, intense sexual preoccupation and frustration, feelings of failure, a sense of futility, and a wish to escape.

The Dance

The vast majority of relationships between men and women begin because men initiate them or *act*, making it possible for women simply to *react*. When men act and women react, a process dynamic is triggered that leaves men feeling responsible and guilty when things go wrong. Despite the advances of the last 40 years for women, this process element between men and women has not changed.

The actor/reactor dynamic is the core reason why men come to feel women are mysterious or impossible to understand. Women who react are not expressing their real selves. Rather, they are accommodating men and adapting to them. Reaction in women generates a sense of being controlled and having their identity denied, regardless of men's intentions. Since being a reactor is reflexive and rationalized by women (i.e., "Men don't like women to initiate," or "It doesn't feel romantic when he doesn't take the lead"), its part in creating the negative feelings women experience with men is denied. Women who react, and therefore accommodate the male's actor role, see themselves as "nice," loving, and victims of his need to control and his ego. "I try to please you, but you don't really care about me," is her reality.

The man-woman relationship process that causes women to be reactors elucidates the unpredictable mood swings and rages women experience with men. As a reactor, when things are not going well, rage over feeling controlled or having no sense of self or self-esteem surfaces. It is impossible for her male partner to identify the cause so she is seen as impossible to understand. She herself does not understand the origin of her moods so she may rationalize that they are biochemical in origin. "Nice" women are dangerous to men because they build intensely negative feelings due to this process factor, and because their process of reaction makes it impossible to see how this dynamic is causing their moods and rage.

Her Experience Understood

- Because she reacts to him, she comes to feel that he is suppressing her identity.
- Because she reacts and accommodates, she comes to feel that her ideas and needs are diminished and discounted by him.
- Because she reacts, she develops low self-esteem, or feelings that she is nothing, nobody, or invisible.
- Because she reacts, she comes to believe that she is unknown to him. "You don't even know who I really am," she tells him.
- Because she reacts, she provides him little stimulation. Consequently, when he is bored or distracted, she comes to feel that it's because he's not really interested in her as a person.

His Experience Understood

- Because he acts with her, he comes to feel responsible for whatever goes wrong.
- Because he acts and makes decisions, he feels guilt and a sense of failure when things don't work out.
- Because he acts, he comes to feel bored and deadened because spontaneity, unpredictability, and novelty are absent.
- Because he acts and experiences no stimulation, he will crave escapes through work, fantasy, withdrawal, and a vulnerability to addictions that allow him to avoid his experience.

Rage in Search of a Reason to Discharge it

The psychological drama played out inside women and caused by their process creates the sudden outbursts of anger, the unreasonable accusations, the depression, the frustration and lack of fulfillment, the excitement of fantasy where the promise of fusion sublimation exists, the feminine paranoia stemming from disowned and projected anger, the rage, and the terror of losing herself behind dissolving ego boundaries.

Because these are byproducts of her process, but are unacknowledged, unrecognized, and denied, she is in search of a reason, or "something out there" to blame for the buildup of horrific feelings. Although the seeds are planted long before adolescence, during puberty they begin to surface and mushroom. To quell and encapsulate her pain and fury, religious obsession, food addictions, chronic illnesses and fatigue, the paralysis of phobias, or obsessive fusion with children or pets may occur.

Her male partner is plagued with a sense of responsibility and the guilt and self-hate that are byproducts of initiating or acting. These beliefs cause him to be "driven crazy" by a growing helplessness to do something to improve the relationship and the distorted belief and notion that he is responsible for her anger and pain, and that he can stem and turn the wild tides. However, the drama caused by a woman's process is self-generated and will be played out with or without him.

A Woman's Process Creates Undue Personal Optimism Plus Unrealistic Fears

After attending a social event, a woman will often make positive comments about the evening and the persons attending. Meanwhile, the man is thinking, "Was I at the same party she was? How could she think those boring people were fun? How could she describe the host as a nice guy or the hostess as sweet? He was such a phony, and the hostess was a self-centered bitch."

While a man's process may produce cynicism, distrust and negativism about the outside world ("it's a jungle"), her process creates the polar opposite: an undue optimism that is viewed by men as naïve and Pollyannaish. At the same time, feminine process also creates undue external fears that bewilder men who can't make sense of a woman's anxiety and panic at seeing a mouse or a spider, going out alone to public places, confronting a dishonest car mechanic, hearing the loud noise of thunder, or speaking up in public.

A man hears a woman say, "Isn't that wonderful?" or "They're so nice," or "That's so great," or "She's so sweet," or "Isn't he terrific!" He tunes these responses out or finds them irritating because they differ so greatly from his own perceptions and reactions. Regarding external, worldly, or competitive matters, he hears from her, "It scares me," "I'm afraid to speak out in public," "What if they don't like me?" "I'll never pass that test," "Please call the airline for me," or "They'd never hire me!" Men respond to these reactions with exasperation and try to talk a woman out of her feelings. "You'll do just fine," or "That's nothing to be afraid of," he says.

Her process causes perceptions and reactions that are not rationally negotiable because they come from the defenses that shape the way she is and how she experiences reality. They are not the product of something thought through. They are how she feels.

Is She Really "In Touch"?

Marianne thought of herself as aware, sensitive, and intuitive while she viewed her husband Charles as clueless. After a while Charles began to believe this was true and that when it came to personal matters his wife was the expert. While it is true that a man's early socialization damages his capacity for awareness in personal relationships, a woman's distortions, lack of awareness, and ways of being out-of-touch are more difficult to see.

"Everybody knows" that men are out-of-touch and in denial of their feelings and effects on others. Goal driven, competitive, and controlling, they don't see their process and what they're really all about on a personal level until it's too late. Because women express feelings more easily and are focused on the personal side of living, it is assumed that they are "in touch" and aware. This is one of the illusions that retard the growth and development of male/female relationships.

The ways she is out-of-touch are many, and include the following:

- She is out-of-touch with her sexism, which is every bit as intense as men's objectification of women. Men are attractive, sexy, and desirable to her to the degree that they are powerful and successful. A man is a success object, who is attractive to the extent that he can be a rescuer, a protector, and a provider. None of these necessarily have any connection to his qualities as a person—the thing that most women believe is their major priority.

- She thinks that she wants intimacy, but it is a subjectively defined intimacy, meaning a closeness that satisfies her needs and does not take into account his reality and process. She thinks she wants intimacy with him, but reacts badly when his reality and inner self are expressed and revealed. The intimacy she believes she wants is based on what she needs and what feels good to her. When she speaks of intimacy, she is not speaking of closeness with who and what he is, but closeness with what she would like him to be. She blames him for not giving her things that it was obvious from the beginning he didn't have in him to give.

- She believes that she is a better parent than he is, based on the perception that her personal needs and process are more intensely focused and intertwined with the children than his needs and process. That enmeshment, however, is no better or worse, only different in its effects than the most out-of-touch man's disconnection from his children. His disconnection unwittingly pushes them away. Her intense fusion prevents them from separating and individuating.

- She perceives herself as loving and spiritual, when, in fact, she carries within her intense rage for which she will blame him. This blind spot adds to the distortion about what his contribution to the relationship problems is versus hers. Her anger and aggression are as intense and destructive as his, though harder to see and identify. Moreover, denial makes it impossible to manage and move her relationships toward the direction of a balanced interaction and negotiation. She sees herself as kinder and more peace-loving when, in reality, her hurtful impulses are acted out indirectly and passively through him. She allies herself with, and is attracted to, the most aggressive, competitive men, who she perceives as sexy and attractive. She becomes the support system that spurs him on in the competitive pursuits from which she benefits. Since these are his actions, she can dissociate herself from them.

- She sees herself as independent and autonomous, but is attracted to and feels romantically toward a man who can take care of her. Men who are not protective or seen as caretakers are not romantically appealing.
- She perceives herself as being controlled by him, yet when he asks her what it is that she wants, she can't provide a clear answer. She makes no connection between her resistance to making decisions and her feeling that she is being controlled and deprived of her identity.

The lack of awareness or being "in touch" in men is usually obvious, while the lack of awareness in women is harder to see but every bit as real and damaging.

The Problem with Traditional Women

People were surprised and baffled when Judy, a seemingly happily married woman of 32, developed symptoms of depression, anxiety, and an eating disorder. After all, she came from an intact family where mom and dad seemed to be ideal parents who loved their children. How could Judy be unraveling and in such pain at such an early age?

People who knew her attributed it to self-indulgence: "She's just spoiled and too into herself," was their interpretation.

Even women and men from loving homes and supportive family backgrounds become dysfunctional and live lives with broken relationships, addictive habits, inevitable crises, and breakdown points, all built into and generated by their gender process. The so-called normal girl and boy are extremely vulnerable to it, and only by identifying, acknowledging, and transforming this process can it be remedied.

When a woman fits the feminine or traditional prototype, certain dysfunctional habits, patterns, and endpoints will occur no matter how wonderful her childhood, and no matter how normal her personality seem to be. *The closer to the feminine ideal, the more dysfunctional she will be in her committed relationship.*

Dysfunctional behaviors that result from her process include:

- preoccupation with her appearance, weight, and diet that can readily evolve into obsessive reactions and eating disorders.
- low self-esteem that she expresses as easily hurt feelings, and that creates self-doubts, indecision, and even depression.
- a loss of boundaries in relationships, which creates intense anxiety over abandonment, a bottomless need for reassurance and contact, and overreaction to emotional distance and relationship problems.
- emotional reactions that readily become screaming, tearful, or raging outbursts. Her internalization process intensifies and the irrationality of her responses reduces her capacity for logical or reasonable discussions of problems.
- an identity crisis that occurs because she loses herself in her roles as mother, wife, daughter, and sometimes friend; she cannot maintain identity boundaries and arrives at a point where she experiences the terror of

having lost herself. She will look for someone to blame, usually her male partner.

- "flakiness" in the form of lateness, irresponsibility, impulsive spending, procrastination, and not following through on commitments.

The word "traditional" tends to trigger defensiveness in women. "What's so bad about being a traditional woman?" is a common reaction mainly because the conversation about being a traditional woman tends to focus on what she seems to be (nice, giving, sweet, loving, etc.), rather than on her process and the way that creates her experience of herself and the way that she relates to others. The more traditional the woman, the greater her blind spots and defensiveness. What she is appears to be attractive, while the actual impact of her process, or how she is with others as well as herself, is the fountain of many serious dysfunctions.

A Blamer is a Blamer is a Blamer

Rudolpho, a thrice-divorced man in his forties, put it aptly: "Relationships with women always begin on a high. When the relationship begins I'm the hero, the rescuer, and superman, all wrapped up in one package. Naturally, it's hot and romantic and the woman adores me. As the relationship progresses and negative things happen, she reacts with hurt, disappointment, or silence. The message is clear: The problem is my fault, it's my creation.

"In my twenty years of experience with various women, I can barely recall a woman who acknowledged her contribution to a problem. The words, 'I'm sorry. I screwed up,' or, 'That's my problem and I want to work on changing the way I react,' are not what I hear."

The health and future of a relationship exists in proportion to the ability of each partner to see his or her own process and contribution to creating its problems and resolving its conflicts. In the traditional relationship, the woman feels victimized and blames her partner, who readily feels guilty and apologizes. This is the inevitable endpoint of the actor-reactor dynamic that makes the man feel responsible and the woman feel controlled and powerless.

Women who blame men in relationships are unaware of and in denial of the ways in which they contribute to and create relationship problems. They are unaware that the very same behaviors they come to resent in men, they initially require of them. Women find men unattractive if these behaviors are not present.

Once the blaming/guilt dynamic is set in motion, it transforms the content of the relationship. Events polarize until the man is always guilty and the woman is always blaming. For him, being in such a relationship is an exercise in self-hate and a sense of failure, as he becomes the target for ever-increasing anger and rage.

When a man first meets a woman, her blaming behavior can be very attractive because it is focused on someone else. This serves two purposes. First, it casts her in the role of a victim of past circumstances. And second, it pumps the man up by casting him in the role of the rescuer or the "good guy." Initially he takes what she says literally and he thinks that he can make relationships and life different for her. But inevitably he will get chewed up by the same process that transformed all of her past relationships. Being a blamer is an expression of who she is, not what has actually happened to her.

The rule of thumb is simply that a blamer is a blamer is a blamer, and there is no way to improve things in a relationship with that being her process without succumbing to defeat and depression. If she has blamed before, she will blame again.

Relating to a Woman: The Best and the Worst of It

The woman seen as an angel, selfless and sweet, may be regarded at other times in a relationship as "a bitch," vicious or impossible. In relationships, how could a man's perception of a woman vary so much? And which of these are the real her? Seeing women in a clear, balanced, and realistic way is crucial to the relationship survival of men.

Women in relationships are much like men in business. When they're at their best, they are upbeat, optimistic, focused, and productive. At their worst, they are ruthless, cynical, paranoid, obsessive, and self-oriented. Since women have been socialized to focus deeply on the personal, they bring the same complex, volatile potential to the personal world as men do to their work. We sanctify the personal and romanticize it as if it were separate from the dynamics that control the other, impersonal or business aspects of life. Women bring the same best and worst aspects to the relationship or personal realm.

The best and worst of women in relationships mirror the best and worst of men in the external realms of money and power. Just as men who are high-powered winners in the world of business have a downside to their personalities that often involves massive needs to control and an obsessive focus on their goals, the same holds true for women in relationships.

At best, women bring a sensitivity, energy, and talent to relationships that makes the personal aspects take life. They can be generous when their partner is hurting and in need, but they can be equally manipulative in a way that a man can't see happening.

At worst, in her relationship behaviors and in her personal focus:

- She can be totally controlling of the relationship, using guilt, manipulation, intimidation, and unpredictability as her major tools.
- Her relationship ego is fragile; she needs to believe that she is always right and she reacts badly to anything she experiences or construes as criticism. Like men with their obsessions about money, sexuality, and achievement, women have fragile and defensive relationship egos.
- She is obsessive about her primary relationships and is easily derailed from other external or impersonal concerns and goals when her relationship security is threatened.
- There is an intense buildup of anger and fear when she is not getting what she needs from the relationship. These feelings may manifest as depression, mood

swings, physical ailments, or food addictions.

- She is paranoid about her love relationship, in that she anticipates the worst and tends to view a committed relationship with a man pessimistically and with anxiety.

- While she perceives herself as desiring closeness and intimacy, she is difficult to get close to except on her terms.

- When things go wrong in relationships, she feels a combination of failure and victimization, much like men do when things don't work out for them in business.

- Because her relationship ego is fragile and defensive, she is easy to manipulate with flattery and positive feedback. She needs and wants to hear it regardless of whether her partner really believes it. It troubles her if she doesn't hear positive statements even if her partner does feel them but doesn't articulate them.

- While she may act sexually responsive and aroused, hers is a fragile interest in sex that can easily be made a low priority. Being loved, not being sexually desired, is her motive.

- She believes that men are ignorant and stupid about relationships. Therefore, she is reluctant to accept input from a man regarding the relationship, even if she pretends otherwise.

- Just as businessmen don't like being away from the workplace very long, she doesn't tolerate distance from monitoring and having reassurance about the relationship. It makes her anxious, just as being away from his business makes him anxious.

- You cannot reason her out of her need for reassurance, just as men cannot be reasoned out of their fears about the future and their preoccupations with the safety and security of their money and power.

- Her obsession with her personal relationships is such that once she starts talking about them, it is hard for her to stop.

In general, the "best" of relating to a woman is the intensity of her focus on the personal. The "worst" of relating to her is also the intensity of her focus on the personal. It is colloquially described as, "You can't live with them, you can't live without them." For most, resolving the conflict between the need and its painful downside is done by rationalizing: "You've got to take the good with the bad." The problem with that rationalization is that with time the bad grows as the good diminishes. Making the personal changes necessary in order to make oneself less vulnerable to the "damned if you do, damned if you don't" bind becomes the challenge.

Why Men Withdraw and Become Silent in Intimate Relationships

"When I first met Allison, I felt like some kind of miracle had happened. She seemed to understand and accept me so completely. I remember the first night of our being together. We talked until the morning. I was so high that as the sun rose I was still completely energized. Flash forward to five years later. I feel tight and self-conscious around her. I guess it was a lot easier talking to her in the beginning because it was about my history and my dreams, rather than talking with her about our relationship. I've slowly given up on that. It's just not worth it. She understood me completely when it came to my past disasters and disappointments, but when I talk about my conflicts and struggles in our relationship the walls come up. She doesn't really hear me anymore. So now I'm either quiet or only talk about neutral stuff. I could just leave notes instead of talking."

Women complain that men in relationships withdraw and don't communicate. This is seen as an expression of a man's relationship dysfunction. What men still don't know is that interpretation is only a part of the truth. What is rarely recognized by either women or men is how the withdrawal and silence are a product of the dynamic between him and her and is at least in part a man's reaction to the helplessness and hopelessness he feels when encountering, on a daily basis, the effects of her relationship process. Unable to engage her in a satisfying way, the only recourse seems to be to close up.

Specifically, the following manifestations of that process are what unknowingly he is reacting to:

Her "Niceness" or Denied Anger

- emerges as unmanageable, passive, and indirect aggression.
- causes her to overreact to anything negative, such as conflict or anger coming from him.
- gives the initial impression that she's nice, yet the niceness doesn't feel good because it's not authentic. He will feel guilty for not being equally nice. The implication is that if he's not as nice, then he is the relationship spoiler and the damaged one.

Her Desire to be Close

- is bottomless: He never feels like he's giving her enough.
- is not based on her desire to be close to the real him, but to the man she romantically fantasizes him to be.
- makes her feel superior because supposedly she is more involved and loving.
- is crazy-making because the harder he tries, the more he seems to fail. The man who doesn't try can simply be blamed for not trying whereas the one who tries and fails is perceived as frustrating, flawed, and hopeless because there is no more hope based on the belief that if he did try, everything would get better.

Her Denied Assertion
- makes it appear initially that she's easy to get along with and that he and she share much in common, but it is actually an inauthentic accommodation that is rooted in her need to avoid conflict, and to have everything be "nice."

- causes her to feel controlled by him and to perceive him as a "control freak."
- causes resentment expressed either directly or indirectly by her over the fact that it's always his way, but when he asks her what she wants or he refrains from making the decisions, she is unclear or confused about what she wants. When further pressured to decide or take initiative, she becomes resentful.
- makes it appear that she is the agreeable and sensitive one.
- causes her to reach an identity crisis where she has the terrifying sense of not knowing who she is or of being "nobody." She then concludes that she will never be able to be herself so long as she is with him, even though he doesn't discourage her from being herself.
- prevents her from drawing and maintaining clear boundaries, which causes her to experience herself as violated by him.

Her Subjective Way of Responding

- frustrates his desire to have reasonable, logical discussions about problems as they come up.
- causes him to retreat in helplessness during emotionally difficult discussions because the more he says, the more she seems provoked.
- causes him to deduce that the only way to get along with her is to agree with everything and to tell her what she wants to hear because anything else seems to upset her.
- causes her to become an emotional blackmailer. Unless he agrees with her, he is blamed for being unsupportive and dismissive.
- causes him to conclude that he is living with a crazy person.

Her Defensive Sexuality

- makes him feel that his sexual needs are at her sexual mercy. Sex is primarily when and how she wants it.
- makes him feel ugly about his own sexuality, and feel as if she is doing him a favor when they have sex.
- causes her to feel that he is pressuring and using her, which adds to her negative and angry perception of him.
- causes her to lose interest in sex whenever other needs of hers are not being met.

Her Intense Focus on the Present

- makes her view him negatively as a spoiler because he "always" focuses on and tries to prepare for future problems.
- creates hopeless discussions in which she accuses him of being pessimistic and having no capacity to enjoy life. In response, he accuses her of being Pollyannaish and acting like a child.
- makes it seem to him that she is impractical and naïve about the future.
- increases his own defensive, self-protective way of dealing with future security because he believes that he has to balance out her impracticality.
- increases his tendency to feel responsible for her.
- creates a chronic tension when she pushes him to lighten up, which occurs as she is behaving in ways that cause him to tighten up.

Once a man withdraws and becomes silent he faces a "damned if you do, damned if you don't" situation. He may be blamed for withholding and being fearful of closeness and intimacy, or if he risks exposing his inner self he may not get through to her as he hoped he would—and often encounters a blaming or guilt-making response. The longer the dilemma remains unresolved, the more destructive it can become. It becomes each man's challenge to solve it because it is a dilemma that will not go away and that sets the stage for the beginning of the end.

The Problem with a Woman's Low Self-Esteem

Arthur cogently voiced a common relationship dilemma and experience men have: "Initially, when I meet a woman who puts herself down, I like to show her how special and wonderful she is, somehow thinking that I can change the way she sees herself for the better. Big mistake! It took me three failed relationships with women who I initially saw so much more in than they saw in themselves before I realized that not only couldn't I succeed, but that it was a draining, neverending process that had to be repeated over and over again and would start to make me feel like an ineffectual loser. The initial desire in me to bolster her was as big a part of the problem as her low self-esteem, which ironically had a pretty intense flip-side. Sure she felt bad about herself, but lo and behold she also turned out to be pretty arrogant. At some point she would start telling me what my problems were and the ways I needed to change. Then, rarely did I hear from her how her low self-esteem was causing her to distort our relationship. Soon she had all the answers for me. It sure got confusing because her issue became my issue and I started to have real doubts about my self-worth."

Part of the Prince Charming–rescuer fantasy that ignites romantic fantasies for men and women is when a man meets a woman who feels badly about herself, he tends to want to make her feel better about herself and her life. He will fail because her low self-esteem is a byproduct of her process and not of external circumstances; specifically,

- Because she's socialized to accommodate and please the man and take on his interests, she comes to feel that she is less than him, or even "nobody."
- Because she's been socialized to value herself for

being and not for *doing*, she is vulnerable to low self-esteem when it comes to achieving and performing. Paradoxically, when she does something well, it threatens her sense of femininity.

- Because she's been socialized to value herself in large measure to the extent of which she is loved and taken care of by a man, she is vulnerable to low self-esteem when her relationship is not going as well as she would like. And, of course, *he* is viewed as her problem.

- Because the symptom of low self-esteem is seen as the culprit, rather than her denied process, a man deludes himself that he can help her feel better about herself. The opposite is true. Instead of improving her self-esteem, his attempts to help will be experienced as patronizing and belittling.

Because the low self-esteem emerges from her process, her self-esteem is not affected by external successes. So long as she reacts or accommodates, or fuses and loses herself in relationships, she will feel bad about herself. A man who plays into that dynamic will be seen as part of the problem, not the solution. The terrible paradox is that by believing that he can play the hero and protector, a man will come to be seen instead as hurtful.

The Very Spiritual Woman

The very spiritual woman is the ultimate Madonna, sparking fantasies in men of having found "the perfect woman," particularly for the man who sees himself as morally weak, damaged, or defective. A man may think that being with a very spiritual woman will raise him to higher levels of spiritual being himself, but the actual reality of the experience is starkly different.

Nowhere is the chasm between process and content, *what* a woman seems to be versus *how* she relates and experiences her relationships, so massive and troublesome. What seems an oasis of comfort to a man when he meets her initially may transform into its opposite as he engages her and the relationship evolves. Unraveling the paradox of the very spiritual woman in relationships makes it possible for men to make sense of the seeming inexplicable—the gap between the illusion and the reality of the experience.

The spiritual woman, like the success-driven man, is full of herself while in denial of that fact. She is controlling, yet sees herself as open and loving. She is toxic in her effect on those who are intertwined with her in a personal realm, while she believes that her effect is uplifting and selfless. Like the success-driven man, she is in a world of her own creation and is impossible for a man to connect with authentically or comfortably because she cannot see herself though the eyes of the other, which makes true relating and loving impossible.

Beware of a woman who is "very spiritual." It may seem positive, but will come to feel the opposite and worse. She may be hidden behind a façade of moral superiority and long-suffering righteousness. Processwise, she may have come to her spirituality because she cannot get fusion needs fulfilled in the world of real relationships. It leaves her in emotional pain and with a lack of personal fulfillment that causes her to turn in a spiritual direction where her craving can be satisfied. Once she has found her sublimated fulfillment in religion or in other forms of spirituality, she will never let it go.

The bottomless fusion hunger, which includes a denied need to lose her self, is transferred to a religious projection object she can adore and trust and which she relates to with full and total commitment because it is without frustration or threat of disappointment and abandonment.

The real meaning of all this is made evident when one observes whom it is that she adores and attaches to spiritually. It may be a manipulative guru, a biblical figure, a role-playing spiritual leader, a therapist, or a "healer." All are people who channel and may even manipulate this hunger.

Attempting an intimate relationship with a spiritual woman is, for her male partner, a journey filled with self-hatred, failure, blaming, and hopelessness. The man who cannot see the process undertow and "tries hard" is left feeling that all his worst ideas about himself have been confirmed. The negative aspects of himself are magnified, such as control, separateness, cynicism, and a sense of being a failure at love.

The specific ingredients are as follows: Her anger and rage are denied, so the burden of guilt for being aggressive falls on him. Her sexuality is controlled, so she has no autonomous overt need, which gives her total sexual power and exaggerates his sense of self-loathing for having a need that she can transcend. Rationality may be blocked in favor of untouchable magical thinking, which means that objective discussion about personal and spiritual matters is not possible. Furthermore, her relative lack of concern for everyday economic reality and demands means that the man who is her partner will be assigned the responsibility for these practicalities, something for which he will not be appreciated, and for which he might even be criticized.

Whatever tendencies the traditional male-female dynamic produces in the way of male self-hate, guilt, and responsibility and the female sense of being the love connection and that she is the victim who suffers abuse, is heightened to the maximum with the woman who has embraced religion and spirituality as her way of becoming fulfilled.

In such relationships:

- He is always wrong and she is right in matters of relationship behavior.
- He is the one who is angry and she never acknowledges her rage and anger, except when she is righteously motivated.
- Only she loves and cares and is compassionate. At best he only tries but can never reach her level.
- She is deep and he is shallow or materially fixated.
- Only she feels the positive or right emotions.
- She is sensitive while he is seen as crude.
- She doesn't really *need* sex while he is obsessive and primitive in his desire for it.
- She is selfless, interested, and caring while he is self-centered and insensitive.

She feels good about herself as a person while he feels flawed and filled with self-loathing. "Everybody knows" that she's too good for him and that she has to put up with so much in order to stay with him. Therefore, she can judge him, while he can never judge her.

Eating Addictions: Food Is Feminine Booze

Traditional men and women have counterpart addictions. For every man who can't stop working and producing, there's a woman who can't stop shopping and consuming. Likewise, for every man with a drinking problem, there's a woman with an eating disorder.

Men's addiction to various substances and the lopsided percentage of male drug addicts and alcoholics compared to women is a well-known fact. What is equally a counterpart addictive expression of women's issues is the significantly greater percentage of eating disorders. According to the National Eating Disorders Association, 10 million women, compared to only 1 million men, have an eating disorder.

Society places negative judgments on men and their desire for beer, wine, and drugs, while it views the equally common women's obsession with and addictive patterns around food as benign or only harmful to themselves. In addition, society often is blamed as the cause for putting pressure on women to be thin.

This dichotomy of interpretation is a variation of the same dynamic that places the blame for relationship dysfunction solely on the male, while the woman's contribution is downplayed or denied altogether. His alcoholism and her food addictions are outward manifestations of opposing but equivalent process dynamics, and are external expressions of the same destructive interactions.

The personal disconnection that fuels a man's alcohol and drug addictions cause him to be personally insensitive and hurtful without knowing it, while her food addiction is part of her dysfunctional process that also fuels her relationship obsessions and many of her anxieties, fears, and distortions.

Women's addictive patterns with food provide a microcosm for observing and understanding the way that their problems in relationships are disguised and invisible while men's problems are magnified and construed as the major causes of relationship problems.

Society reinforces these distorted interpretations that a man's behavior is the cause of the destruction of relationships while her contribution is benign and minimal in impact and effect. Programs for adult children of alcoholics are everywhere, yet there are no programs for adult children of women who had food addictions, with the attendant confusion and craziness they create.

Men Wonder Why: Common and Not-So-Common Questions Men Ask about Women

Due to what men still don't know about feminine process, and to men's tendency to try to understand women's relationship behaviors using logic and reasoning, there are certain mysteries about women that usually lead to stock answers: "Don't try to figure women out," "Even Freud acknowledges he was baffled by women," or the pop psychology cliché that women are from a different planet.

Once we identify *how* a woman translates and responds to relationships based on the defensive filters that underlie her feminine behaviors, the explanations for even the most baffling of her responses become possible. These mysteries turn out to be predictable endpoints of the way that she relates as opposed to what she seems to be on the surface. The following are some recurring questions men have about women.

Why are women obsessed with commitment?

Women need commitment as a goal to motivate them in relating to men, just as men use sex and sexual interest as a goal to motivate their interest in relating to women. Once involved, women need to feel there is movement or potential in the commitment direction, just as men need to feel there is movement in a sexual direction. Once it becomes clear to her that commitment will not happen, she loses interest or motivation to continue the relationship, no matter how "wonderful" the man may be or how much she has professed her love for him.

Why are women moody?

Feminine process involves the blocking of anger, assertion, sexuality, and autonomy in the service of being nice, agreeable, close, accommodating, caring, loving, and nurturing. Consequently, there is denial of the buildup of not-nice feelings and responses such as anger, conflict, feeling controlled, and loss of identity boundaries that creates a tension and hypersensitivity in her that regularly erupts. The more intense and traditional her process is, the more powerful and irrational the outbursts and mood changes. These eruptions of anger and sadness have a clear connection to her blocked feelings. The periodic eruption is the moodiness commonly attributed to her biochemistry.

Why are women negative about men, particularly since men traditionally have a code of chivalry and a protective attitude toward women?

Women's negative feelings about men have many sources. On the one hand, they are a projection of their own denied anger and aggression that causes women to see men as far more angry, abusive, and dangerous than they are. Because they don't counter men's negativity or aggressiveness when it *is* there, this projection leaves women feeling mistreated.

Women are internalized by feminine process and develop needs for closeness and an idealized conflict-free love that are impossible to achieve. Men are blamed for deliberately not wanting to fulfill those needs, for holding back love, and for not making the relationship a priority. Women believe they are deliberately being dismissed, discounted, and denied and it causes resentment.

To the extent that women react to men and give them the power to initiate and determine the direction of a relationship, feelings of powerlessness cause women to feel controlled and even abused and victimized by men. Women's reactivity is rationalized ("Men want us to be that way") and denied ("I am being my own person"). When women feel controlled, abused, or victimized, they believe that their experience is the objective reality. They cannot see themselves as contributors to this experience.

For all of these reasons, the good and loving things that men do are minimized and even seen as self-serving, while the negatives or flaws are amplified.

Why isn't she more objective and rational in her relationships, since she has an advanced degree?

It is a shock when men discover that highly educated, professional women are emotionally irrational in their close relationships. If their process is traditional, meaning they *react* rather than *act*, in their relationships with men, the buildup of intense, denied neediness as they navigate their careers means that once in a relationship, their reactions may be far more extreme even than women with less education and career training. A person's position in the world is no prediction of rational behavior in a committed relationship.

Why are women so fearful?

Women tend to be afraid of things, from mice to spiders, to taking risks or asking for what they want directly, in the same way that externalized men deny fear because they are threatened by labels such as sissy or coward. The direct expression and experience of aggression or anger is blocked and is part of what gives women a sense of being "nice."

It doesn't make sense to see successful and athletic women act scared over a mouse, a spider, loud noises, or confronting their auto mechanics, without understanding the depth and power of feminine process in shaping a woman's emotional experience and how that transforms her power side into inhibition and fear.

Why do Women Ask Men to Open up and be Honest About Their Feelings and then React so Badly, Often with Tears and Retaliation, When Men do?

When a woman asks a man to open up about his feelings, she believes that what he is holding back are tender, vulnerable, loving, and sensitive emotions that she believes he is afraid to show. The feelings that men are actually hiding are feelings they believe women will react badly to or will misinterpret if expressed.

Men sense that likelihood correctly. When a man is seduced into opening up and being honest, he is received badly because the feelings he expresses are not what she expects or needs to hear. It destroys her romantic fantasies when he reveals his true inner feelings. It is foolish for men to take literally the request by women to "Tell me what you really feel," because along with reacting badly, women also tend to hold on to the negatives they hear. In the end, they remember them as having been a major assault on the love that had been in the relationship before he spoiled it.

Why do women lack a sense of humor with men, so that they can't tell when a man is only joking or kidding?

Freud taught us that the basis for humor is repressed hostility. Women overreact to men's attempts to be funny for a combination of reasons. They see or sense the hostility that men are in denial of when they joke. This hostility is amplified through her process: Women, who crave warmth and total love and support, are wounded by men's clumsy efforts to be funny.

The combination of feminine oversensitivity and men's denied hostility creates a tendency toward perceiving men's humor as hurtful and insensitive.

Why do women wait for men to initiate and take responsibility for courtship?

Women rationalize that they feel romantic when pursued, and that men reject assertive women who take the initiative. On a deeper level, however, women react rather than act in part due to what they learn as little girls, namely, they are most lovable for *being*, not for *doing*. Therefore, when they act rather than react they feel less feminine and lovable.

A woman's power with a man derives in part from the manipulation of his defensive need to control, to "show off" and take responsibility, and by the guilt he feels when he fails or makes a mistake. By reacting, women get men to take responsibility for the decisions. They then have the power that comes from making a man feel good (like a hero) or bad (like a failure) by the way that they react to him. Once women take responsibility for initiating and participate overtly in steering the direction of a relationship and its decisions, they lose that power. Asking a woman to take power and control in a relationship is equivalent to asking a man to relinquish it. Both experience similar resistance.

Why, when she does liberated things like offering to pay her part of the dinner bill, does she still act like a traditional woman?

Like the woman who occasionally initiates a first date, offering to pay part of the dinner check is a false gesture if it is a statement, if it happens only at the beginning, and if it has the qualities of something unusual or out of the ordinary. Is she putting up a pretense by paying, or is it an authentic and comfortable response?

Smart women today know that it makes them seem more appealing if they offer to pay their share, much like the man who offers to wash dishes after dinner. Is it real, or is it liberated seduction or posturing? That is the crucial question.

Liberation is not gestures or attitudes. It is genuine non-defensiveness. The latter means that no matter what is done, it can comfortably be discussed without guilt or self-consciousness.

Why do women believe that men want to undermine their efforts at success and independence?

The causes involve both men and women. Men's responsibility exists to the extent that they have intense (denied) dependency on their partners, who are usually their personal lifeline. When a woman becomes successful and independent in her career, there is a threat to her partner that she will no longer need him, and he will be abandoned. To the degree that a man does not really have a relationship based on intimacy with a woman but is a "provider-object," that fear in men is accurate. When a man can't control a woman by providing for her, he has to create a personal basis for the relationship, which he may believe he can't do.

At the same time, her process creates a resistance to sustaining aggressive, goal-directed pursuits toward success and there is a sense within her that her attractiveness and power are lost in the pursuit, of worldly success. Consequently, there is conflict and a tendency to undermine this pursuit, though women will deny their complicity in their lack of success and for which they will blame men.

Because feminine process causes women to be **reactors** and to be internalized, they blame men for things that go wrong for them in the competitive world. The basis of radical feminism, in fact, is the belief that men are women's oppressors and abusers and responsible for the bad that happens to them. Further, women's feelings that men deliberately lock them out of the corridors of power result from a denial of women's avoidance and resistance to the impersonal, disconnected, cold, goal-focused, and aggressive behaviors that are required to maintain competitive levels of success. Women on the verge of high-powered careers and achievement often retreat because of relationship or parenting priorities. The cold, manipulative, and impersonal world that men in positions of power live in is particularly toxic to most women, who crave a community of closeness, caring, and noncompetitiveness.

Why can't women stop talking when men plead with them to, and when men make it clear that they don't want to continue a discussion?

Women can't *stop* for the same reasons that men can't *start* when a woman pleads, "Talk to me!" While men resist vulnerability and engagement, women become anxious in the face of separateness and a closing off of the personal. When women open up, they gain a momentum that is hard to stop, just as men have to struggle to come out of themselves in order to make personal contact once they withdraw into themselves.

Why does sex seem like fun and excitement at the beginning, and then becomes less so and even boring within a committed relationship, particularly when women really want the sex?

While sexual gratification is satisfying, the fun and excitement for men comes from the objectification of a woman, the resistance and the challenge she presents, the validation of the male ego when she consents, and the fear that she might refuse if she is displeased or angry, and might never want to do it again.

However, in a committed or ongoing relationship, particularly when a woman presses to get her needs met, objectification and challenge are eliminated. She becomes a real person with real needs and demands, and is no longer a fantasy to pursue. His denied needs for dependency and closeness are also being met, so most of the sexual motives that drive him as a single man are absent.

Why is she into shopping, and why does she want to buy more when she already has enough?

Women are obsessed with shopping (consuming) for the same anxiety-driven reasons that men are compulsive about working (producing). For men, working reduces their insecurity over performance and power even when they don't have to because they already have enough success and money. Masculine process is focused on achieving and producing because it validates him as a man. Consuming or purchasing validates femininity. Traditionally, women feel loved and taken care of in proportion to what men will spend on them or what they themselves buy or consume.

When men get anxious about their worth, they use work as a tranquilizer. Women use shopping to make themselves feel better when their self-esteem is low. Shopping and consuming are feminine tranquilizers, quelling the buildup of inner tension, just as working and being productive are men's tranquilizers.

Why does she say that I scare her and that she's afraid of me, when I would never do anything to physically hurt her?

A woman's fear of men is caused by a combination of the repressed and denied anger that she projects and sees as coming at her instead of from her, and the defensive aggression in men that is denied and that defends against and blocks his vulnerability. Instead of vulnerable emotions being expressed, traditional men act distant and even irritable when they feel hurt or needy. That combination causes men to seem offensive and threatening even when they would never become violent. Many men seem to be angry most of the time, but don't know it and deny that they feel that way.

Why do women believe that men can't love?

Women experience love as a fusion or a progressive movement toward greater closeness, where there is an absence of resistance and conflict and an ever-increasing focus on being together. Men are not capable of fulfilling these needs because their process moves them in the opposite direction. Men believe they can love and be separate and that doing for rather than being together is a valid demonstration of their love. Men are bewildered that these manifestations of love are not perceived as such.

For men, love tends to be an abstraction or idea that can be fulfilled through action. For women, it is a feeling of increasing closeness and a melting of boundaries or separateness. Therefore, when women believe that men can't love, they are going by their feelings and not by men's intentions or actions.

Why does she tell me that I'm selfish and self-centered, when I do so much to make our relationship a priority?

Women's perception of men as selfish and self-centered has two sources. The first is men's process, which causes men to be in denial of their bottomless needs to control, to be right, to preserve their space, to compete, and to prove themselves. The emotional impact of these on the woman is one of self-centeredness and selfishness.

The second source of women's belief is the feminine process that causes them to experience men in a distorted way, namely, to exaggerate the negatives while discounting the positives (the non-selfish, non–self-centered things he does). Her process in relationships involves dissolution of the self plus a tendency to accommodate, which creates in women the sense that they give, give, and give, while men only take.

The objective giving or not-giving may be equal in a man-woman relationship, but the way women give and the way they process and perceive relationship reality creates in them the sense that they are the giver and the ones who are selfless, loving, and concerned, while men are selfish and self-centered. While this is a gender illusion created by the polarized way that men and women defend themselves, it does create the overall impression of the loving woman and the selfish man.

Why does a woman get breast implants in spite of the health warnings, risks, and protests of the man she says she's doing it for?
To understand the "craziness" behind why women get implants, men need only look at the counterpart process compulsions that cause men who have had heart attacks to continue in their self-destructive, driven, workaholic patterns in spite of the health warnings, or the men who continue to play sports when injured and in pain, and who take unnecessary risks and challenges that may harm them in the name of "being a man." These "crazy" things women and men do don't make sense unless viewed from the perspective of powerful process-driven forces, anxiety-driven motivators that make performance and success for men feel like life-and-death matters.

Women's sense of being valued, attractive, and secure comes from feeling that they are physically attractive. Studies have shown that losing weight ranks among the most satisfying thing that can happen to a woman. If having implants creates the feeling of being attractive, then women will deny the risks of doing so just as men will readily risk their health to do things that validate them as men.

Why can't I tell if I can really believe and trust her?
Because men are externalized, they interpret trust as a concrete abstraction rather than as part of a dynamic. If trust means predictability and a negotiated agreement, a woman's process dynamics in interaction with a man's makes women unpredictable because:

- women build resentment over feeling controlled.
- women are not in touch with negative feelings, and therefore these feelings don't get expressed directly, nor does conflict get resolved. Thus, anger may emerge at any time in unmanageable, irrational ways.
- women's low self-esteem is projected so they see their partners as putting them down even when that's not men's intention. This causes women to react unpredictably.
- women's lack of assertiveness and boundaries gives

them the sensation of not having a self. They believe it has something to do with their relationships and they blame men for that.

- what women promise is based on their feelings at the time and these feelings are sure to change.

Why does she say I control her when that's the last thing I want to do?

This results from a combination of the intertwining of women's projection over resisting taking control and men's denial over being controlling. Women resist taking control and blame men for that, while men tend to avoid relationships they can't control and tend to deny that.

Why does she always want to talk about the relationship?

When it comes to personal relationships, women are as obsessive as men are about sports, stock market prices, net worth, careers, and the like. Women are always taking the temperature of the relationship the way that men regularly check the value of their financial portfolios. Women are always feeling the danger of their relationships collapsing, just as men readily fear their financial and power world toppling.

A question about women acting sexy that men rarely ask, but really should: Does dressing and acting sexy mean that she actually is sexy and enjoys being sexual?

It probably means the opposite. If she dresses and acts sexy, what it most likely means is that she is manipulative with men and uses the bottom line and what usually works to control them or to get what she wants.

If a man drives an expensive car and flaunts his success symbols in front of a woman, does it mean that he enjoys spending money on her or supporting her? More likely, he uses his money and success symbols like women use their sexual symbols, to attract a woman and to fulfill his agenda, which is probably sexual or possessive in nature. Once he gets that, he no longer wants to spend his money lavishly, if at all.

Distinguishing content from process helps determine what is really going on in man-woman relationships. For a woman, dressing "sexy" is content. How a woman uses her sexuality is process. To make sense of her reality, the question is, why does she behave as she does, not what is she doing? Authentically sexual women don't need to dress or act "sexy."

3 **What Men Still Don't Know About Relationships**

✓ *The Romantic Way:*

» *The Romantic Date*
» *The Masculine Role: Why it doesn't Work in Relationships*
» *Predicting the Endpoints of a Relationship from its Romantic Beginnings*
» *Romance as the Relationship Drug*
» *In Romance, Men are Mother Substitutes*
» *Romance and Its Consequences*

✓ *Understanding The Communication:*
» *Women's Addiction to Fusion (Women Call it "Intimacy") and Men's Addiction to Disconnection (Men Call it "Freedom")*
» *How Men and Women are Similar, but in Opposite Ways*
» *Why are Women Angry at Men?*
» *What Women Feel with Men*
» *Why Women Don't Apologize for things They've done, While Men Apologize for things They Didn't Do*
» *What Women Say about Men ain't Necessarily So*
» *When You are Not what She Says You are, Although You'll Never*
» *Convince Her of That*
» *Whose Feelings are They Anyway?*
» *Talking about Gender Needs doesn't Work, it Only*

Makes things Worse

✓ *Seeing the Relationship Realistically*:
  » *Women Have an Agenda Too*
  » *What Women Say about Men*
  » *Early Warning Signs of Polarization*
  » *When She Needs You, You Can't do Anything Wrong; When She doesn't, You Can't do Anything Right*

✓ *When It Looks Like Love, But Really Isn't:*
  » *Does Love Between Men and Women Really Exist?*
  » *When Traditional Women Fall in Love*
  » *Is it Intimacy or is it Exploitation? How to Differentiate the Two*
  » *Are Men Women's Clients?*
  » *Why Women are also Incapable of Intimacy*
  » *When it Looks Like Love*

✓ *When it Looks Like Love, But Really Isn't:*
  » *A Portrait of the Toxic Relationship*
  » *Knowing When to Leave*

✓ *Unravelling the Mysteries:*
  » *When Women or Men don't "Get It": Making Sense of Relationship Addiction*
  » *When Nice Guys are Hated*
  » *Hopeless Pursuits: Futile Relationship Efforts by Men*
  » *The Abused Male*

The Romantic Way

The Romantic Date

Any personal moment in time, when minutely observed, examined, and analyzed, can tell us what is happening, what the players are about, and where a relationship is going. "The Date" is such an event. The interaction, the feelings and responses, the expectations, the games, and the way decisions are made and conflict is dealt with, present a microcosm for what will go wrong when the fantasy and euphoria of the new and the romantic fade.

A traditional date is, in pure form, a playing out of the *actor* (masculine) / *reactor* (feminine) dynamic. Few dates occur, or continue to occur, unless initiated by the male. In spite of the rhetoric of feminism and the men's movement, and beneath the surface of politically correct attitude changes and intellectualizations about gender roles, little has changed in male-female courtship. Even the most career-minded, ambitious, and successful women rarely initiate their dates. When occasionally they do, the ball is quickly passed to the man and traditional patterns take over once the relationship is launched.

With few exceptions, men still are the first to request the telephone number, make the first call for the date, propose an evening to go out, drive the car, select the restaurant, pay the bill, take responsibility for carrying the brunt of the conversation, decide what to do after dinner, and read the signals for sexual play. The only thing that has clearly changed in the last 30 years is that most women decide for themselves what to order in the restaurant. As the actor, he becomes responsible for the experience of the date and therefore feels guilty if the evening and its events aren't pleasurable. As an actor, he is actively creating the experience almost by himself. The reality of the interaction is, therefore, often boring for him because he receives little input or stimulation, but he will be blamed for acknowledging his boredom, assuming that he is aware of it.

"The Date" is work for the man because it is his responsibility. It is his task to entertain and pay for the attention and affection of the woman. The dynamic undertow creates guilt and self-blaming in him, if not self-loathing, particularly if he is strongly attracted to the woman and does not manage the evening successfully.

The content is the *what* of the evening, the details of that which will transpire. The process is the *how* of the interaction, the dynamic between him and her. It is the process that will create the deeper feelings or inner experience for both. For him, the process is responsibility, self-blame, and self-hate if things go wrong; guilt when mistakes are made; and a sense that he must perform and perform well if he is to win the attention and affection of the woman. If all goes well, he feels validated and euphoric. But these feelings are ephemeral and contingent on his continuing good performance.

As the reactor, she waits for him to initiate. For her to be validated, she must *be*, not *do*. She must be in a way that is compelling enough to get his attention. If she doesn't, her self-esteem is lowered. The process impact is that she cannot act and therefore feels powerless to create her experience assertively. Therefore, traditional women are obsessed with their appearance, their physical and social image—that is, their power. Her process is to react and her inner experience is to feel controlled and powerless.

Once a date is made, the woman's power and control derive from being indirect and manipulative. What she really wants, she must maneuver him into giving. The subtler her style is—to the point of it being invisible—the better. Her other process role is to accommodate him and make him feel good about his choices.

To be direct and assertive is to be unfeminine. Instead, she must be pleasing and agreeable. If he is making decisions and seems enthusiastic, she must find a way to validate him. Therefore, the process or undercurrent that develops in her, regardless of the content of the date, is that he is in control of the decisions and his choices shape the events.

This tells us two things about her developing feelings. As a reactor, she will come to feel controlled and also feel that she has no intrinsic identity or self in the interaction. Her identity on the date solely comes from reacting to him.

When the magic of dating is over, what she is left with are feelings that:

- *He controls me.* The anger over that will deepen with time.
- *I have no identity when I'm with him and he has robbed me of it.* To get my identity back, I will have to leave him or get angry and rebel.
- *His will, desires, and ego dominate and he dismisses and discounts my feelings.*

These process endpoints are set in motion on the first date— only they are not acknowledged. Rather, it is taken for granted that this is the way it is done, and initially it may even feel good. The endpoints have little to do with the content of the experience. That is, it doesn't matter how "nice" or "not nice" a man is, or how "strong" or "liberated" a woman is. The process (how) of their interaction will transform and eradicate the content (what).

An analysis of the first date can help us predict everything that will ultimately go wrong in the relationship. In the dynamic of the date, he must objectify her either sexually or as a nurturer to make it interesting for himself because she is not behaving as an autonomous person. His excitement comes from his fantasy of her, how he can possess her. He is also an object to her because of the way she relates to him. He is an object who has the power to make her happy or unhappy with his choices, and can rescue her from her problems and make her life better.

The Masculine Role: Why it doesn't Work in Personal Relationships

As the actor, with her as the reactor, he will be responsible and carry the guilt for what goes wrong.

- As the autonomous one, he will be perceived as undermining the closeness.
- As the assertive one, or the take-charge decision maker, he will be seen as controlling.
- As the detached problem-solver and fixer, he will be experienced as cold and unfeeling.
- As the practical man who concerns himself with money and the future, he will be seen as the one who doesn't know how to have fun and who is cheap.
- As the protector or aggressive one, he will be the one whom others fear because he "scares" them.
- As the one who is focused externally and takes on the primary role of dealing with outside responsibilities, the children will not bond with him, and he will be the one from whom they feel alienated because he is not fully present with them like mother is. They may appreciate him at best, but they won't feel close to him.

When things go wrong in his intimate relationships, he may look to find the reasons in something that he did or said, or didn't do or say. What men still don't know, the elusive truth here, is that it's *the way they are*, based on the role of a man, that produces the inevitable end results and not the everyday minutiae that they comb through to try and unravel the mystery of their failure.

Predicting the Endpoints of a Relationship from its Romantic Beginning

Looked at from a process perspective, it becomes possible to see where a relationship is going and where it will land. What men still don't know is that the way a relationship plays out and is experienced by both parties involved is determined by the *how* of the relationship, or its process, and not by the *what* of the relationship, or it's content. In that sense, any advice based on what to do is misleading. *In the traditional relationship it is possible to do everything right and yet have it turn out all wrong.*

The what, or outward content, of a relationship determines

its course primarily in its early romance phase when how a woman looks or what a man does to please his partner have potency. As the relationship evolves, how it feels to be with the other person takes center stage and begins to transform the relationship. Initially, if a man is generous and comes up with interesting things to do, it may make him appealing. In time that fades into the background and the feelings are generated by the way that it feels to be with him.

Similarly, the woman who is beautiful and sweet may be compelling to a man at first. However, his experience of her will soon be determined by the way that she relates. Does she blame him? Does she have a clear sense of herself and is she able to generate ideas and input? Is she able to set boundaries and be clear about what she wants? When there's conflict can she negotiate without seeming to be devastated? Does she cry and act as if she's been badly wounded?

The ending of every traditional relationship is the same: namely an angry, blaming woman and a guilt-ridden, self-hating man. It doesn't matter if she is a CEO and he is a kindergarten teacher or poet. The how of a relationship, not the what, creates its deeper dynamics and its endpoints.

Because the process dynamic is the major influence in shaping the emotional experience of a relationship and because it creates the ongoing, consistent pattern of the interaction, the direction a relationship is heading can be predicted from the extent of these dynamics. The more polarized and extreme, the more rapidly and intensely will the endpoints be created.

If he is the actor-hero and she is the reactor-pleaser and accommodator:

- She will experience him as controlling her.
- She will feel she has lost her identity to him and that he doesn't value her input.
- He will feel that he is responsible for everything.
- Her anger will become bottomless; eventually, almost anything he says or does will trigger it, until finally the relationship dissolves or she becomes depressed and sick, as he withdraws completely in order to escape a

situation that has gone out of control and that feels terrible.

- He will come to feel bored because of a lack of stimulation and he may even start to act in resentful, abusive ways without knowing why, because of that boredom and sense of being weighed down by the responsibility to make her happy.
- She will increasingly feel that he should take care of her because he can. He will come to feel burdened and smothered.

If he "rescues her" and she romanticizes him and tells him how wonderful and different he is than other men:

- Once she is "rescued" (married, taken care of economically, free from an ex-husband), she will start to see the "real him" and will become critical and disappointed. He will be confused because he knows that he hasn't changed; her perception of him has.
- The exciting sex that is triggered by his having been placed on a pedestal as the knight in shining armor and rescuer will dissipate and become progressively less exciting as she starts to withdraw.
- She will pull away from him as she starts to feel stronger and more autonomous and she will resent him if she believes that he wants her to remain the adoring, helpless, and vulnerable partner she was in the beginning.

If she tells him how abusive men in her past have been, and he takes it on himself to prove to her that he is not like those men from her past:

- He will come to treat her in ways that are similar to how she was treated by the men in her past. This is because she did not see herself as part of the problem and will resume the same provocative behaviors with him and he will react accordingly.

- She will come to be resentful of him because he "tricked her" into believing that he would be different.

A Final Thought on Men's Obsession with Sex and Women's Obsession with Intimacy

A quick indicator of a relationship's lethal polarization potential is the degree of focus and preoccupation with sex in the man and with intimacy in the woman.

Intimacy is a byproduct of growing mutual liking, trust, and understanding; it is not a need to be filled. Similarly, a man's obsession with sex signals the degree of his tendency to objectify women and use them for tension release in a depersonalized way.

Men who are immediately obsessive with a woman about sex, and women who wonder immediately about the closeness or intimacy potential with a man she has spent little time with, are already polarized. Tension will build because he can't really give her what she needs, and she denies these limitations. Furthermore, unlike him she can't give herself comfortably for mere sexual pleasure, which will create continual conflict.

Such relationships begin romantically with intense sexual activity and a man's declaration of closeness, which disguise the potential for enormous conflict in the near future. Both will feel frustrated, but men will be primarily blamed and held responsible because men's obsession with sex is easily criticized, whereas women's obsession with intimacy is positively interpreted.

Romance as the Relationship Drug

A substance or experience that creates a sense of euphoria that transcends and overwhelms rational thought is said to be addictive. It distorts reality, giving it an allure that is objectively unwarranted. Painful, interfering realities are suppressed and forgotten as the craving returns and builds. One's better sense is impotent in the face of the desire for the drug.

"The higher the high, the deeper the crash," is the formula I use to understand and predict the course of passionate, romantic beginnings as they follow the inevitable progression from romance to boredom to rage.

Those who fear and resist the opposite sex the most are most in need of intense romantic beginnings in order to transform the threatening reality into a magical event that temporarily provides a release from isolation and despair. This irresistible beginning allows for a short-term fulfillment of needs and escape from one's inner longing and frustration.

Romance resembles the experience created by an addictive drug in that romantics repeat the same cycle in each of their relationships—with increased speed and a lack of learning—until they crash and burn and give up on ever finding what they think they want. As with addictive substances, the initial experiences are very exciting and mind-altering, taking them to euphoric heights with no concern for or attention paid to longer-range consequences. Instead, there is a wide range of variations on the denial theme, from "This feels so good it couldn't be bad," to "It's worth it. I'll worry about the consequences later." Romance acts like a drug and has similar mind-altering powers, creating euphoria, release from tension, impaired judgment, and distorted emotional reactions ultimately culminating in a damaging end. The reality behind them is revealed by the fact that, not uncommonly, people in so-called great romances have little to no interest in seeing each other once the romance is over. Without the drug of romance, there is little to hold onto.

Like all drugs, romance has its greatest power to alter experience in the beginning. Later, increasing doses are needed merely for maintenance, while the euphoria is hardly even felt, and lasts only a short time.

Over time, after a number of failed romances, the pattern is played out more quickly and to further extremes. A relationship that would have taken years to run its course gets played out in a month or even a passionate weekend where the excitement on Friday night turns to anger and disappointment by Sunday.

Because of the polarized defenses and realities of men and

women in traditional relationships, the gap of understanding over mutual hurt and the fear of the trauma being repeated cause the reality of relationships to become laden with a negative charge. Thus, as the gap between men and women increases, the vulnerability to and hunger for magical romance increase along with the resistance and fear.

In Romance, Men Are Mother Substitutes

The unknowing relationship template women carry in their psyches has its origins in their relationships with their mothers. In their friendships and love relationships, they try to reproduce that same original intensity. During the romantic phase, when a man's fervor and passion are at a peak, a woman may believe that she has accomplished it. As romantic intensity diminishes, women become frustrated and disillusioned at the lack of intimacy they are experiencing. The more intense their relationship with mother had been, the greater their need for closeness with a man will be.

This may lead to despair and bitterness toward men as men repeatedly fail to provide the closeness women crave. There is no realization on anyone's part that a woman is trying to reproduce the feeling of closeness she had with her mother. Without realizing this, she is doomed to go from man to man in search of fulfillment. A married woman will live with frustration and longing that will cause her to seek substitute fulfillments.

Romance is powerfully appealing to a man because its magical energy and intensity and the instant, total love the woman gives him provides a reprieve from his own relationship issues and shortcomings and the isolation they create. There's no effort or work required of him. She does it all through her fantasy projections. The price for the euphoric initial fantasy is paid at the back end.

The best of romance comes earliest. As the relationship progresses, it turns to emotional chaos and at the end comes a release of rage on the woman's part that matches the initial romantic euphoria in intensity. When it's over, it's often worse than being strangers with her, because strangers have some tolerance for each other. He is often left disoriented and bewildered; one step closer to being fully convinced that women are crazy and it is hopeless to be in a relationship.

The man who is the recipient of the initial romantic rush would be dismayed to realize that he is a mother substitute in a man's body. He is the outlet for the sum total of process problems, distortions, and fears that the romantic woman acquired through her own fusion with her polarized mother, a mother who turned to her for the gratification of intimacy needs she couldn't fulfill with her husband. It looks like this: mother's dysfunctional process is visited upon the daughter. Daughter then attempts to simulate the fusion-intensity of her relationship with mother, combined with a need to be taken care of, protected, and supported because she fears she can't do it herself in a world controlled by men. When she thinks she has found the absolute best of both worlds, a man both capable of intense fusion and who will also be a wonderful provider and caretaker, a frenzied romantic passion is unleashed. A man's response to the romantic and sexual aspects initially makes it seem to her that he is as fusion-capable as she is.

Fusion-mothers—women with intense closeness needs who use their children as outlets for their quest and to escape from the frustration and pain of relating to their husbands and who appear to other people to be wonderful and devoted mothers—addict their daughters to a standard of intimacy and a craving for closeness that can never be experienced with a real person, much less a high-achieving, externalized, "real man."

Because women addicted to intense fusion are poor candidates for ever providing consistently for themselves, the period of initial romantic euphoria comes as a result of the intense chemical mix of the woman's projections and her longings to be taken care of. Her process defeats that aspiration. The best of her skills are transformed and eroded by the feminine process of intense emotionality, fear, and need to fuse herself with another person. These process hungers interface with and obstruct the goal-oriented, externalized focus required for sustained competitive success and its financial rewards. While she may have the abilities it takes to make it in the economic world, she can't sustain the effort to build and maintain them.

She projects her fantasy of intimacy and being cared for onto a man she believes has the credentials that make him a winner. She then creates a self-defeating, self-fulfilling prophecy. That is, she gets an intensely romantic response initially in return, but is misreading a man's excitement over the instant, intense sexuality, adoration, and accommodation to his every wish and desire combined with his ego-delirious state resulting from being told and made to feel that he is the most wonderful man on earth. He responds powerfully to her romantic adoration that has made possible the instant and intense sexuality and fantasy that he craves and that causes him to pay attention to her in an obsessive way so she can believe, temporarily, that he desires and can satisfy the intimacy she needs. Yet he cannot, and the bubble will burst soon after he is locked in.

Often, the first person she tells about him is her mother, who is ambivalent in her reaction: happy for her daughter's happiness and for his potential as her caretaker (because mother and daughter are one), but unhappy because she is losing her daughter to him. Subtly and unconsciously, she will chip away at the relationship from the sidelines, even as she acts as if she supports it. When daughter sooner than later comes to her in tears and crushing disappointment over what he did or didn't do, said or didn't say, mother will be there to comfort her, take her back in, teach her about what men are really like, and to counsel patience while she confirms the sad reality that, "Yes, men are insensitive, self-centered, hurtful jerks." "Try to understand him," she tells her.

Inevitably, daughter will be painfully disappointed as the romantic fog created by her own projections and his response to them lifts, and the rage of betrayal and frustration builds. Initially, the pain of the relationship will alternate with interim periods of trying to recreate the euphoria through sex, sentimental and tearful promises, and resolutions to try harder. However, this interim period is impossible to sustain.

She is addicted to a fusion craving, and he can never come close to fulfilling the closeness craving, and she has no idea of her own contribution to the problem. After all, she believes that she just wants to be loved. The relationship crumbles with her feeling let down, misled, victimized, betrayed, hurt, and abused. He was nothing like her mother; in fact, he turned out to be the opposite. The more she demanded closeness, the more he closed up.

After a healing period, she will begin a search for the next romantic fantasy. She is a romance addict, but cannot recognize or acknowledge the source of the problem and pattern. Other people feed her fantasy that somewhere out there she will finally find the man who can fulfill her dreams. After all, someone always knows someone who supposedly has. In the meantime, she will become a desperate, haunted person, doomed to burn out and become bitter and enraged at men over her repeated failed romances. On the way to the final burnout, she will repeat the cycles of initial excitement, chaos, anger, and despair until perhaps she doesn't want to, or cannot do it anymore. Food, religion, soap operas, and ever-available mother will become her substitute for fusion craving and romance with men.

The man who enjoys the initial sexual passion and holiday from reality that a woman's romantic projections provides would find it difficult to believe that behind his pumped-up ego, he was only a temporary substitute for her mother, an emotional fix in a man's disguise—which is why all of her supposed sexual lust for him disappears in a moment when she realizes that he cannot give her the intimacy she longs for.

If his masculine ego is as needy as her fusion cravings, he too will become addicted to the intensity of the initial romantic euphoria, and will seek out other women with fusion addiction to experience again the initial high. The man who becomes addicted is most likely a "momma's boy," or a fusion-addicted male, in search of a repeat of the fusion intensity he had with his mother as a young boy.

That is why romance is so powerfully irresistible to those who crave it, so chaotic as it plays out, and so painful, disappointing, and draining as it repeatedly ends, until finally it leads to a sense of hopelessness and despair over ever finding a relationship that works.

Romance and Its Consequences

- Feeling romantic, she sees him as being much more

than he is, or different than other men, which is inevitably followed by a backlash resulting in her seeing him as much worse than other men and totally flawed. Romantic fantasies feed the male need to believe he is different and better. However, the "more of a man" he is, the more she'll become disillusioned as the illusion of difference wears off and she realizes that he's just like other men.

- Along with romance comes intense pressure to get closer and commit. One gets pulled in or seduced by the feeling of being so loved. During romance, a man is vulnerable to committing without fully realizing whether he really wants it.

- Romance creates intense pressure to deny conflict and anything negative. The covert contract is to pretend everything is wonderful. The relationship builds an undertow of blocked feelings that will inevitably seep through in many indirect forms and periodically erupt in overreactions and explosions that make him think that he is going crazy.

- Romance brings out the maximum feminine anxieties in her, the bottomless quest for reassurance, the tendency to lose her boundaries and her identity, her desire to want everything to be nice, her tendency to blame and feel hurt and abused, to cry when she is angry, and to see herself as giving much more than she is getting.

- The inevitable progression of romantic beginnings is from romance to boredom to rage.

- Because she is so "nice" during romance, it tends to intensify a man's tendencies to feel responsible, self-hating, and guilty when there are problems. Soon it becomes difficult to distinguish whether he loves her or just feels responsible for her and guilty for not giving her what she wants.

- The man gets blamed increasingly as problems arise. Just as he was larger than life when she met him and needed him, he becomes lower than low when she's ready to pull away. Extreme distorted accusations occur, sometimes even hideous ones such as "You've tried to rape me," "You're abusive to the children," "You're inappropriately sexual with our daughter," "You're dangerous," etc.

The process that underlies romance is not conscious, deliberate or premeditated. Still, men need to become conscious of what it is that they are helping to create for themselves.

Understanding the Communication

Women's Addiction to Fusion (Women Call it "Intimacy") and Men's Addiction to Disconnection (Men Call it "Freedom")

The most distressing and painful dialogues in relationships are about women's feelings of not getting the closeness they need, along with men's desire for space. In relationships, men's need for distance and women's need for closeness emerge from their denied gender process and are not needs that can be controlled or even moderated without a profound level of self-awareness, a realization of the unhealthy and self-defeating nature of these compulsions, an understanding of how they are expressions of one's gender conditioning, plus the willingness and courage to go through the anxiety and threat to one's gender "comfort zone" as one works to break through these powerful inner process pulls. Left alone, they turn out to be bottomless and create a vicious self-fulfilling spiral. As the need increases in one partner, it triggers the equivalent opposite in the other. This leads to polarized conversations in the nature of "You never want to be close" (her), and "I feel like I'm being suffocated" (him), or "I always feel you're distancing me" (her), and "I never feel I can satisfy you or make you happy" (him).

If a woman's traditional need for intimacy, or a man's traditional need for freedom or space were anything close to what it is alleged to be, or simply a conscious, controllable preference, men and women would have little problem understanding and trying to satisfy those needs in each other. However, what each gender senses in the other is that "intimacy" and "space" are euphemisms for a bottomless, rigid, and defensive pull that emerges from gender defenses and produces pain, frustration, resentment—and ultimately a sense of hopelessness in one's partner, who believes it can be changed, or at least modified, if the genuine desire and good will to do so was only there. That's where each partner's anger comes from. "You wouldn't distance me if you really loved me and wanted to be close" (her), or "I have to constantly prove myself and my love to you. I feel like I'm not enough for you and it makes me feel like giving up" (him). Inevitably, they come to be polarized by what initially seemed to be understandable and acceptable demands. What brings the relationship to its knees is the inability of each partner to see their own part in this mutually reinforcing and accelerating cycle. Specifically, each pull away by him produces an equivalent desire for more closeness from her. Her pursuit of more intimacy produces his reciprocal self-protective and defensive withdrawal.

The defensive nature of each is denied by each person, though it is painfully obvious to their partner. When women talk of intimacy, men know either directly or intuitively, that it is a need they can't fill—something that they will fail at and then be blamed for. Similarly, women know that the buzzword "space" disguises an impenetrable wall that becomes more deeply entrenched and forbidding when it is gratified.

Initially, each tries to give what the other wants. Trying only highlights the hopelessness of the quest. Without trying, hope for change can continue to spring eternal. However, when he announces that he is trying to work on his "closeness problem" or she deliberately works at giving him more space in order to please him, the forced unnatural nature of their efforts only makes everything feel that much worse. So much for the prevalent psychological belief that all behaviors can be negotiated. These deep needs can't simply be negotiated away. A show of trying will only highlight the hopelessness of the situation until one or the other finally announces that they can't take it anymore or undermines the partnership by seeking relief from the tension elsewhere.

It would be a constructive beginning, however, if women

acknowledged the toxic fallout they produce by being closeness and intimacy addicts, and if men acknowledged the toxic fallout they produce by being disconnection or separateness addicts, unavailable for genuine personal connection.

So what are men and women in relationships supposed to do? Foremost is the importance of not denying or attacking the experience and perception of one's partner. Secondly, it requires the ability to recognize the defensive gender pull in oneself and acknowledge it. "I think I know that what you're always telling me is true. Yes, I can feel myself doing exactly what you're saying that I do. If I don't work through it with you I know that I'll just do the same thing with my next partner, and maybe worse."

Denied and defensive gender process and the many ways in which it distorts and filters men's and women's experience of reality and themselves is, I believe, the next frontier for gender transformation in the so-called gender revolution. Its ramifications go far beyond the relationship between men and women, and it is exhilarating to envision a world in which these distorting prisms no longer discolor and toxify human experience. One can barely imagine what life would look like once the polarized defensive realities of men and women no longer had control and produced the self-destructive compulsions that are at the core of so many of life's mysteries and tragedies.

How Men and Women are Similar, but in Opposite Ways

Truly, women and men are flip sides of the same coin. They are psychological counterparts, no better nor worse, manifesting patterns derived from opposite sides of the gender continuum. The undertow is moving in opposite directions. The relationship reality becomes polarized and defensively distorted equally by both.

To the extent that men objectify women, women objectify men. To men, women are "sex objects"; to women, men are "success objects." Men's agenda is sex and freedom; women's agenda is closeness and commitment. Both have needs that move toward bottomless, "never enough," and opposing directions.

Men's true feelings tend to come out after sex (or after they get what they want), at which time they tend to lose interest in the person of the woman, withdraw, and become critical and even hostile toward her. Women lose interest and become critical and hostile after they get what they want, which is permanent commitment in the form of marriage, at which time complaining about him begins.

While men get bored with and have trouble sustaining interest in women's conversational focus on relationships, feelings, and personal happenings, women get bored with and have trouble sustaining interest in men's conversational focus on sports, business, sex, cars, and money.

Just as men lose interest and withdraw from a relationship once they discover that they will never get what they want (i.e., sex), women lose interest once they determine that they will never get what they want (i.e., commitment or marriage).

Men have trouble identifying women's softer, vulnerable emotions and feelings and tend to replace them with anger and distance. Women have trouble identifying negative feelings such as anger, needs for space, and desire for control, and replace them with vulnerable ones such as fear, longing, and a desire to please or for closeness.

When women are serious about relationships, they are as grim, humorless, ego-involved, and intensely focused as men are when they are serious about their work or competitive pursuits. On the other hand, women tend to be as tenuous in their business and competitive pursuits as men are in their committed relationships.

Contrasting Gender "Truths"

- Men fall in love when they get their egos stroked and expanded (filling all space). Women fall in love when they can dissolve their egos (identity) and fuse (lose) themselves in a relationship.
- Men have answers to questions and issues they know little about, and they're convinced that they are right. Women feel ignorant and incompetent in matters where they may actually know a lot, but they're convinced that they don't.

- Men get angry when they feel vulnerable. Women cry and act vulnerable when they really are angry.
- Women often use PMS as a rationalization for out-of-control behavior like men use getting drunk to avoid responsibility for the expression of parts of themselves that they disown and choose not to accept responsibility for. Men like to believe in biochemical rationalizations for behaviors that would allow for a cure with a pill or other treatment. We are not the mere products of biochemistry, our deeper self is only magnified by it.
- Women often cling to relationships and act dependent even though they are actually very separate. Men often act separate in relationships when they are actually intensely dependent.
- In relationships, women may act irrational when they actually know exactly what they're doing and what's going on. Men act rational and as if they are in control of the relationship and know what's going on when in fact they are in the dark.
- Men interpret personal interest on the part of the woman as sexual. Women interpret sexual interest as personal.

When they hit the wall of reality, each feels deceived and used, though each was only a victim of their own need-motivated distortions.

Why Are Women Angry at Men?
A thoughtful and introspective man, Andy nevertheless found himself bewildered by the outpouring of rage from women when they spoke honestly about their feelings and perceptions of men. "Most men I know seem to go out of their way to please women, and when they fail they usually feel guilty and responsible. Then when they find themselves confronted by women's horrific anger that comes pouring out at them, they wind up concluding that either women are crazy, or that making a woman happy is an impossible thing. On the face of it,

it just doesn't make sense. Most guys I know would sure love to get a handle on this."

It is not so much what a man does, but the interplay between feminine and masculine process that produces rage, frustration, and diminished self-esteem in women. What men still don't know is that a woman's experience is built-in and a byproduct of feminine process. It has nothing to do with how nice or not nice he is, nor with what his intentions are ("I'm trying to be loving and sensitive").

Feminine process generates a longing for fusion or closeness in women that makes a man's quest for autonomy and separateness frustrating and painful. Feminine process generates a longing for niceness and conflict-free relationship harmony that masculine aggression and lack of vulnerability frustrates. Feminine process causes emotions to be women's primary reality filter. Men's logic and quest for objective truth and negative reactions to emotional expression cause women to believe that their reality is being undermined and diminished. Feminine process generates a longing to be close and together that men's compulsive need to do and to structure time with activities frustrates. Feminine process creates intense emotion and needs in association with the sexual experience that men's quest for novelty, and fantasy in sex frustrates.

When a woman reaches a breaking point and anger comes pouring out:

- she feels she can't take the denial of her needs any longer.
- she feels she can't take being diminished or put down anymore.
- she feels she can't take his "abusive anger" any longer.
- she feels she needs to be with someone who really wants to be with her.
- she feels she can't take his coldness, negativity, and detachment any longer.

At this crisis point, men look for logical reasons to explain the breakdown. They believe they tried their best and that should outweigh the problems. The answer is not in what he did or did not do, but in how she feels with him, and the needs that are chronically frustrated. Even in the end, the gap in understanding continues.

What Women Feel with Men

What men still don't know is why women are so focused on and obsessed with commitment in their relationships. It is simply because a casual, noncommitted relationship to a woman feels much like a relationship without sex does to a man. He may put up with it for a while if he profoundly cares about the woman, but the tension in him builds to the point where sex is always on his mind and becomes his controlling obsession.

To a woman, a man's detachment and absence of emotional expression feel much like the woman's uncontrolled, explosive, endless emotional ranting does to a man. It doesn't make sense to a man that a woman reacts so negatively to his abstract, cold demeanor. Nor does it make sense to a woman that a man would react so negatively to a woman's expression of intense emotion.

To a woman, little to no affectionate touching feels as distressing as being endlessly touched by her does to him. To a woman, a man's planning for economic security way into the future feels impractical and unrealistic, just as living totally for the moment's gratification monetarily by buying whatever one likes does to him. A man's being obsessive about his work and career feels to her much like a woman being obsessive and relentlessly focused on the relationship feels to him.

The content of a relationship is the illusion and the hope. The gender process is the reality that repeats itself endlessly and defeats us ultimately, unless it is acknowledged and transformed.

Why Women Don't Apologize for Things They've Done, While Men Apologize for Things They Didn't Do

Martin, a newly married man, was describing a recurring and troubling pattern in his relationship: "I always apologize when we have an argument or blow-up and somehow she never does. I'm partly to blame because somehow I feel that she doesn't need to.

I'm just glad that she's not angry with me anymore. Somehow I always feel guilty—like I did something wrong, even when I really know that I didn't. Maybe it's because I believe that she's more involved in this relationship emotionally than I am and therefore in some way, or because of that, I'm really always at fault because I don't care enough."

A distressing byproduct of men's process in relationships is the feeling men have that they are always somehow responsible for the relationship problems. In part, men feel relationship inadequacy because they were not raised to make relationship competence a skill to value and develop.

A distressing manifestation of feminine process is that it causes women to experience hurt and abuse where none was intended or even visible. Because men are the *actors* or initiators in the relationship and the carriers or overt expressers of aggression, men are cauldrons of easily triggered guilt and self-hate. Thus men apologize, even when their partners' accusations don't make sense.

He says, "I'm sorry if I didn't sound really supportive of your plans," "I'm sorry if I didn't see how hurt you were over your sister's comment," "I'm sorry I didn't realize that you only wanted to be held and didn't want me to touch you sexually. You seemed so excited," or "I'm sorry if I sounded critical when I commented on the outfit you were wearing, but you really did ask me what I thought."

By contrast, a woman will do things that are discourteous or insensitive, such as breaking a date at the last minute, arriving late, procrastinating and causing her partner to be late to a social event, expressing raging moods at inopportune occasions, refusing to go with him to a social/business commitment at the last minute, spending money beyond the budget, forgetting to do a promised errand, or falsely accusing him, all without apology or a sense of the effect of what she's done.

The feminine process dynamic of reacting, and not expressing aggression, control, autonomy, or sexuality in a direct and active way generates in women a sense of righteousness, and victim rage. Within the male-female relationship, feminine process does not generate the internal sense of being responsible or guilty, so even when women do apologize, it is not accompanied by a sense of self-hate or guilt. These apologies, however, tend to be rare, because in traditionally polarized relationships, women's sense of being victimized, abused, and frustrated is so pervasive that they rarely see a justification for apology.

What Women Say About Men Ain't Necessarily So

Men hear assertions and accusations, which may have the ring of truth—but distorted truth. Upon closer examination these assertions turn out to be partial truths, at best.

"Men don't open up." Men do open up, but when they expose their feelings and inner reality, often they are met with negative reactions that cause them to decide that the way to relationship survival depends on their hiding. It is not that men can't open up, but that women can't listen non-defensively to what men experience and would love to tell them.

"Men don't know how to love." Men love no better or worse than women, only differently. Men are focused externally, so they express love by doing for and taking responsibility. This does not fit women's definition of love, which is internally focused and has as its standard an ever-increasing quest for closeness that men cannot provide and satisfy.

"Men don't like women." Men look to women for most of their personal fulfillment and are less critical, angry, and harsh in their appraisal of them. While it is true that few men can see or relate well to women as people, that limitation exists among men in all their relationships, with each other, with themselves, and with their children. Men objectify themselves and other men based on performance and function, not on being, because that is how they've been socialized. However, their preoccupation with and desire for a loving female partner is undeniable.

"Men are afraid of closeness." Men need the closeness of women. However, external pressures for performance and success short-circuit their personal capacity and how close they can allow themselves to get without making themselves feel at risk of becoming too vulnerable or soft. The equation of dependency with a lack of

manliness causes men to mask their need for attachment behind a façade of autonomy.

"Men resist and are afraid of commitment." While this assertion may be correct in the initial phases of a relationship, a man loses his resistance to commitment as the relationship progresses. Today, it is women who end the majority of relationships. Once men allow themselves to trust and commit, they tend to stay.

When You Are Not what She Says You Are, Although You'll Never Convince Her of That

"She tells me I don't make her feel special."

"She tells me that I don't make her 'feel like a woman.'"

"She tells me I don't really care about our relationship."

"She tells me I only think about what I need."

"She tells me I don't tell her what I'm feeling."

"She tells me I'm full of anger and it's the only emotion I ever show."

"She tells me that she doesn't feel important in my life."

"She tells me that I don't appreciate her."

"She tells me that I'm not emotionally supportive of her."

"She tells me that I'm critical of her."

"She tells me I discount and devalue her."

"She tells me that I ignore her."

These are the bewildered and frustrated statements made by men who have tried their best to be a sensitive, caring partner. They worry and obsess over what she thinks and they seek her approval before they make almost any personal plans. They rearrange their own interests and needs to give her interests and needs priority, but somehow that doesn't come through enough to impact her responses and beliefs. While she may begrudgingly acknowledge that her partner tries, it doesn't make her feel loved and cared about.

Men make the mistake of rationally trying to convince their partner that what she is saying isn't really true, and they do that with specifics and facts about what they have done for her. It doesn't work. It has a comparable effect to a woman trying to prove that she really isn't dependent, or unrealistic, or too involved with her children when a man believes she is. She feels it, so it's not negotiable or even changeable. It doesn't make it true, even though it is the truth to her. It's her reality filtered through her feminine process way of experiencing.

The objective reality is somewhere in between men's denial of their alienating impact (how they come across to those who are close to them and aren't aware of) and women's distortions created by their defensive feminine process that leads to projection and exaggerated perceptions. Specifically, if she represses her anger and lives in a defensive world of "nice," she will perceive a man's anger as far greater than it is. Other people's "nice guy" is her angry, cold man.

If she has insecurity about her competence and her ability to compete in society, she may see even helpful suggestions by him (that she invites) as being criticisms, put-downs, and undermining comments. If she has intense, albeit denied fusion (intimacy) needs, she will see her partner as not wanting to be close to her. The greater her denied need, the stronger her sense that he won't get close.

If she has great needs to be central in people's attention and to have continued validation from friends, and so is often on the phone, she will see him as critical if he comments on that. If she is indiscriminately positive and supportive because of her blocked aggression and anger, which can be seen when expressions such as "nice," "that's so terrific," "she's such a beautiful person," and "that's wonderful," continuously appear in her sentences, she will readily see her partner as unsupportive or critical of her even when he reacts with what he intends as helpful input.

These feminine process dimensions make her believe she is right as she unwittingly distorts his responses; it will feel that way to her regardless of what the objective truth is, or what he believes that he is doing or intending. No amount of explaining himself will change her feeling.

Whose Feelings Are They Anyway?
Little kids do it when they interact and play. They accuse each other of things that actually characterize something they are in denial of.

They may say, "You're a little baby," "You're a liar," "You're a scaredy cat," or "You're a sissy." They see in their playmates what actually exists in a denied part of themselves.

One major reason male-female relationships start to feel so crazy is the denial and projection of disowned feelings and impulses by both genders. Men feel pressured and irritated by women's focus on the relationship, yet it is the man who centers his personal life on his female partner, and it is he who is threatened by her autonomy and readily gets jealous if her attention is directed elsewhere. Women have networks of personal relationships and are far less dependent in that way than men are.

Women accuse men of hating women. Yet who regularly spits out the hateful notions that men are pigs, jerks, rapists, sexists, and not to be trusted? Most men are reverent around women and would kill for their mother or wife's honor. Women accuse men of being controlling, yet most men are happy to be left alone and for the woman to pursue her own interests and to make most of their relationship decisions. "Whatever makes you happy," he is quick to say. At the same time, women readily pull men's guilt strings if they don't get what they need or want, and women discourage their partner's non–work related activities that don't include them.

Men describe women as crazy or irrational, rarely reflecting on the insanity of how men act impulsively and destructively with other men for no rational reason. They choose a partner based on her smile, hair color, or breast size, and pursue the intimacy of sex from women they barely know. But after they attach and commit to a woman, they almost stop talking to her.

Meanwhile, most women are eminently sane and practical in the way that they choose a man as a partner and how they go about attempting to create a relationship. Once a relationship ends, most women reveal themselves to be totally rational as they go about legal proceedings and creating a new life. The so-called logical man often descends into desperate measures to hold on or to fill the empty spaces of his life.

It is instructive that both genders tend to see the other in negative ways that involve descriptive adjectives such as, "liar," "crazy," "not to

WHAT MEN STILL DON'T KNOW

be trusted," "controlling," etc. If anything, both genders are projecting their own tendencies that neither want to nor can take responsibility for. It is easily seen by others because, as these assertions are vented, the distortions are pathetically obvious. It would serve both genders well to acknowledge their own insecure, irrational, and dishonest ways in the intimate relationship. Instead, most relationships are stuck in a groove where each rationalizes their own negatives then projects and magnifies them in the other.

Talking About Gender Needs Doesn't Work— It Only Makes Things Worse

Pop psychology, self-help books, and even practicing psychologists promote the notion that honest communication is a step toward making things better between a man and a woman. However, because the needs men and women have in relationships often have dysfunctional, unhealthy, and defensive origins, they are bottomless and alienating.

She says, "I need more closeness." He says, "I need more space." He says, "I need more excitement in our sex life." She says, "I need to be told you love me more often and I need you to just hold me."

The problem with discussing gender needs: We can only ask for what we're aware of. The true nature of gender needs is in denial. A man believes he needs more freedom, but because of deeper blocked anxieties, this need for distance is fear-based and bottomless. Similarly, she may think she needs more closeness, but her deeper need to fuse and get closer and closer until there is no separation in order to quell her anxieties is also defensive, anxiety driven, and bottomless.

Initially men and women believe that they're being loving by trying to fill a rational need in their partner, when in fact, the need is defensive and bottomless. In time each sees the "never enough" nature of the need in the other, but not in themselves. The bottomless nature of the needs causes men and women to fear and resent each other and to use the adjectives "never" and "always."

The true nature of these needs comes through in the spontaneous language couples use when they fight. She says, "You *never* want to be close. You *always* want to be off doing things alone." He responds,

"You can *never* leave me alone, even for a few minutes. You *always* have to be in my face. I'm *never* enough for you."

Each feels unfairly attacked and responds, "What do you mean, I *never*! What about last time . . . when . . . ?" The distortions of "never" and "always" are actually *not* a distortion on a deep level, where the truth of each other is sensed. Indeed, the denied disconnected part of him *never* wants to be "close," while the deeper fusion craving part of her *never* wants separateness.

Attempts to negotiate bottomless needs are common in relationships. They promote despair and feelings of futility and hopelessness instead of resolution or compromise. She says, "You were with me but I know you really didn't want to be." He says, "Even when you leave me alone, I can tell it bugs you and I feel like you're angry about it."

Communication about these gender needs is frustrating and painful because so much is in denial. Men and women can see that denial in the other, but not in themselves. When partners confront each other with (she says) "You're *always* irritated when I talk to you" or (he says) "You're *always* blaming me for something," they're both correct but flying in the face of denied gender process. Instead of helping, these dialogues irritate and provoke and lead to defensive, damaging, and alienating dialogues.

What men still don't know is that trying to please their partner when it runs counter to one's process inevitably fails. The efforts come across as phony, mechanical, and forced. "You're doing it but you don't really want to!" one's partner senses correctly. These dialogues deteriorate and become reciprocal accusations that make each partner feel a sense of hopelessness about making themselves heard, understood, and recognized.

Since both genders tend to exaggerate the alienating behaviors of the other, a constructive, non-defensive starting point would be for each to acknowledge the significant grains of truth in the perceptions of the other: "Yes, I do get resentful and bored quickly if I can't have things my way" (he), or, "I know I readily feel insecure, abandoned, and rejected if you do things that don't include me" (she). Short of being able to acknowledge this, each needs to at least question their own self-defeating tendencies to use words such as "never" and "always" in full knowledge that their only effect is to drive the other into a deeper sense of despair and hopelessness about the relationship.

Seeing the Relationship Realistically

Women Have an Agenda, Too

One of the illusions of romantic relationships is that men have an ulterior motive, such as sex, while women only want to love and be loved.

What men still don't know is that women, like men, don't notice or become attracted to a person of the opposite sex unless they have a clear motivation. When it becomes obvious to a woman that the motive will not be fulfilled—like men when they discover they will not get what they want—her interest and love disappear.

Foremost on the agenda is to be in a committed relationship leading to marriage. That all-encompassing motive may have any one of many sub-motives, including:

- wanting to be rescued from a frustrating life situation.
- wanting to get away from controlling parents or an unsatisfying relationship with a man she is involved with.
- wanting to be taken care of, financially as well as emotionally. Specifically, wanting someone to protect her from the things that she fears. These include being alone and responsible for herself, making decisions, dealing with money matters, or dealing with the everyday stresses and conflicts of life.
- wanting to be validated as lovable and attractive.
- wanting a baby.

Is there anything wrong with having a motive? The correct question is not whether the motive is right or wrong, honorable, or deceitful. The issue with a woman's motive is that it unconsciously transforms the man into an object, just as with men who have an ego motive in wanting to be with a "beautiful, sexy woman." She is attracted to him for his potential function in her life, a motive she will deny because she wants to believe that her motive is pure love. Hers is a denial no different from a man's denial when he says, "I really do love you. I'm not just after sex."

When she denies her deeper motives, an important element of the reality of the relationship goes into denial. She is feeling "deep, loving feelings" that are actually defensive and unreal, or without a foundation of love, albeit appealing and believable.

Consequently, at some time after she achieves her motive—perhaps shortly after marriage, or years later when there are already two or three children—the real feelings begin to emerge directly and to take center stage. At that point, a man feels blindsided and bewildered. He can't believe or understand the sudden change, as her former love becomes instead anger and accusation. By that time, he can do nothing to alter, appease, or reverse her feelings, because the relationship had no foundation of real love in the first place. He cannot call on the old loving feelings to divert or soften the angry, rejecting ones, because the old, loving feelings were part of a defensive denial process designed to facilitate whatever her original agenda had been.

Men are equally responsible because of their resistance to looking at the true nature of the relationship in the first place, along with the need to believe the unbelievable—namely, that they are irresistibly lovable just for being themselves.

Men who are the most vulnerable to these disastrous relationship transformations are the men who are highly competitive, arrogant, and out-of-touch with anything personal. They need to believe that love can be instant and effortless. The more complete this macho arrogance element, the more painful and turbulent the subsequent relationship experiences will be, and the more convinced he will become that women are crazy or impossible. Actually, the "crazy" was his belief that the unbelievable can happen, namely that an attractive woman can fall instantly in love and find him irresistible. "Crazy" is not so attractive later when it does not rescue him from his denied relationship incompetence and destroys his dream.

What Women Say About Men

The following is a sampling of anonymous responses given by women at various gender workshops when they were asked what they do not openly disclose to men:

- "It upsets me that he often seems so helpless and dependent on me, and that he thinks I'm the dependent one."
- "It drives me crazy when he lectures and gives me speeches about things, often when all I want is to be listened to."
- "I get tired of hearing about how men need space and freedom, especially since they act like such dependent babies once you get involved with them, and then when you leave them alone."
- "Men's resistance to just being straight about what they feel and where they're at drives me crazy. They just withdraw."
- "I feel sorry for most men. They seem so empty, so lonely, so insecure."
- "I wish he'd have more friends and not be so dependent on me."
- "I'm really only interested in material things when I'm with a man and nothing else is happening. Most men just don't know how to relate, so I start thinking about food or something trivial."
- "Men's preoccupation with having sex right away strikes me as so weird, and a little repulsive. I like sex, too, but I prefer it with a real person."
- "Most men don't know how to relax and have a good time. They seem too damn serious, and about so little."
- "It makes me laugh how self-important men get when they talk about politics or the economy, as if their opinions were so important."
- "Most of the time when I talk to a man, I don't feel he's really listening, and that is such a turn-off."

- "I wish he'd be more romantic: kissing, touching, and talking to me. The 'silent man' is really hard for me to take. It's too weird."
- "It's hard to believe men when they say 'Nothing' to the question, 'What are you thinking?'"
- "A sexy man is a man who knows how to talk, especially if it's personal and not about his work."
- "It makes me laugh when I hear a man say his wife is his best friend, especially when I watch him with her, and he doesn't even seem to know who she is or how to talk to her."
- "When I hear a man say he's working for his kids and his wife, I feel sorry for him. He'll be in for a shock when he finds out that the kids can't stand him because he doesn't know how to relate to them, and doesn't even know who they are."
- "Men must have pretty big egos to think that they could spend weekends watching TV and hardly talking, and that women will somehow love them for that."
- "Don't men ever stop thinking about money?"
- "Men are too uptight about sex. I wish they'd lighten up about their erections and stuff like that. A sexy man to me is a man who's comfortable with himself and knows how to be playful."
- "Most men seem so negative, so critical and cynical, and they really believe they're right all the time."
- "Mainly, I need him to listen. When he gives advice, I feel like he's disgusted if I don't take it. The way he tells me makes me not want to do it."
- "Men tend to think women are unrealistic because they don't worry about twenty years from now. When I see men worrying about the future, I think, 'What future? He must be kidding himself.'"
- "If men don't like women to cling, I wish they'd stop acting like they can do everything."
- "Men think I want to take away their freedom. All I

want is a relationship with someone who knows how to care. Most men who worry about their freedom don't seem to know how to relate, even when they are there."

- "I am bored by most men. I'm smarter than they are, and I can control them easily. I enjoy having control over my own life."

In relationships, it often seems like women are two people. One is the person they seem to be with their partners, while the other is the person they are when they're apart from men. The tendency to hide and disguise is encouraged early on through the social instructions to "act feminine."

For most men, there is a sense that they allow themselves to be fooled and lied to in order to maintain their illusions. However, the end result of women's hiding the negatives is that these negatives grow until they can no longer be contained and so come bursting forth in unimaginable and destructive ways. When that happens, men are equally responsible for the ensuing damage by having colluded with the woman's need to pretend in order to hold onto their own need to deny the reality of the woman's real feelings.

Early Warning Signs of Polarization

Because a woman's process largely determines her experience of and feelings in a relationship, it is possible to predict the potential problems and their severity by how a woman relates. Observing the how allows a man to cut through the initial romantic fog so that he can avoid being blindsided. Initially, a relationship may seem to be wonderful even when it is already heading for disaster. Or, a relationship may be ragged and seem ordinary at first, but if the process is healthy it has the potential to grow into something special.

The following are the early warning signs announcing that no matter how good things may seem to be, they're moving in an unhealthy direction.

The Warning Sign: She uses the word "nice" frequently and reacts to conflict, arguments, or negatives with tears and withdrawal.

The Consequence: She will be a blamer and will perceive herself as a victim and her partner as the hurtful, insensitive one.

The Warning Sign: She's so easy to get along with, it almost seems magical. Everything he wants to do, she seems happy with.

The Consequence: She will come to feel controlled by him, and will feel as if she has lost her identity or self in the relationship.

The Warning Sign: She tells him how wonderful he is, and how different he is from other men.

The Consequence: If she needs to romanticize him this way, she will react badly and with disillusionment when she discovers the "real him."

The Warning Sign: She is happy to become part of his life immediately, almost as if she had no life of her own before he entered it.

The Consequence: She is looking to escape from herself through the relationship and will become intensely dependent on it and deeply insecure about losing it.

The Warning Sign: The word "commitment" comes up for discussion early in the relationship.

The Consequence: She is objectifying and relating to her partner based on what she needs and whether she thinks she can get it, and not who he is. She will react to him in an angry and threatening way if her quest for commitment is stalled.

The Warning Sign: It's hard to think of things to do besides eating out, going to movies, and having sex when he's with her, and even sex is not very appealing.

The Consequence: The relationship will come to feel stale and boring, and he will be accused of losing interest in the relationship and being hurtful and insensitive.

The Warning Sign: She never gets angry except when she's blaming him.

The Consequence: Her anger will be experienced from a righteous victim position, which he will be blamed for causing.

The Warning Sign: He feels guilt easily around her, as if everything that goes wrong is his fault.
The Consequence: When a man feels guilt easily, it means that he feels solely responsible for what goes on. In addition, he is allowing himself to be manipulated and to take on the role of "the spoiler."

The Warning Sign: He feels he has to censor his thoughts and feelings to maintain the good feelings. In other words, he feels he has to tell her what she needs to hear.
The Consequence: When a man does not feel safe revealing himself, he will have to keep an emotional distance that he will then be blamed for.

The Warning Sign: He gets distracted and bored when she talks to him.
The Consequence: He will begin to seek out ways to avoid being with her. She will feel rejected and hurt and he will feel that it's his fault for not wanting to be close.

The Warning Sign: Bad feelings erupt unexpectedly over trivial matters.
The Consequence: She is building anger that he will be blamed for that periodically leaks through.

The Warning Sign: She doesn't feel good about herself and wants him to support her emotionally in plans and ideas, even when they seem unrealistic to him.
The Consequence: When he cannot do it, he will be accused of undermining her self-esteem.

The Warning Sign: Many things frighten her.
The Consequence: She will seek protection and look to him to take increasing responsibility. When he resists, she will lash out in anger.

The Warning Sign: He always has to end conversations because she doesn't. Likewise, he has to let go of an embrace because she doesn't.

The Consequence: Because he has to set the boundaries, he will be accused of caring less than she does.

The Warning Sign: She has little to no savings, and she owes on her credit cards.

The Consequence: She is unrealistic about finances, and she will look to him to compensate for her money woes.

The Warning Sign: She loves shopping.

The Consequence: The craving, or method of making herself happy, will become his responsibility. When he reacts in anger or with irritation, she will blame him for being hurtful, cheap, or critical.

The Warning Sign: She talks of diet and food often.

The Consequence: Much of her focus will be on herself and the nightmare of eating obsessions will speed up over time.

The Warning Sign: She worries a lot about how she looks.

The Consequence: She will look for constant reassurance that she is attractive, and when she doesn't get it, she will react with hurt and insecurity.

The Warning Sign: She is often asking for reassurance that he loves her.

The Consequence: Her quest will become tiresome and cause him to withdraw, which will lead to him being accused of not loving her. A self-fulfilling prophecy will have been set in motion.

Process factors make it possible for men to see where a relationship is going long before its inevitable endpoint. Consequently, men can alter the relationship's course by changing the way that they participate, reinforce, or allow the trends to continue. At the worst, they can avoid being blindsided. At the best, they can work to correct trends for the good of the relationship.

When She Needs You, You Can't do Anything Wrong; When She Doesn't, You Can't do Anything Right

What men still don't know is that a woman's feelings toward him may have little to do with anything that he does. At the beginning of a relationship when she needs him, it matters little what he does so long as he fulfills her need for commitment. She will forgive and overlook anything. Similarly, when she is ready to end a relationship, the slightest behavior will be amplified to justify that desire. At this point, men torture themselves searching to understand what they did wrong, or what they can do right to change her mind. Most times, this effort is futile and lethal to a man's self-esteem; when her need to be in the relationship is gone, nothing he does can alter the course.

For men to understand this more clearly, they need only think of times when they lost interest in a woman, sexually or otherwise. Did her efforts to be more sexually appealing or to please him trigger a revival of his desire? Probably not.

The excitement a woman immediately feels when she becomes romantic or "falls in love" is related to the needs she seeks to fulfill rather than the reality of the man she falls in love with. It is much like a man who pursues sex from a woman and disregards her potential negatives and hazardous qualities because he is driven and controlled by his need. She puts the man on a fantasy pedestal, perceives him as different, and temporarily overlooks or rationalizes away the negatives. Friends can't dissuade her, no matter what warnings they give.

He may sense that her loving eyes are inflating him, but his ego wants to believe that he is as wonderful as she says. It feels too good to challenge her distortions when she tells him how excited she is about him.

Once her needs are met, like the sexually sated man, her perceptions of him begin to change. Men put it this way: "After I married her, she started to try to change me and became critical of everything about me." Not only does he fall from the pedestal, it becomes open season for criticism, complaints, and blaming. As perfect as he seemed to be in the beginning, that's how flawed he becomes in her eyes after her needs (for commitment, support, babies, etc.) have been met.

In these experiences, a man's enemy is not the woman, but his own grandiose ego that leads him to believe the unbelievable—namely, that he is this wonderful, one-in-a-million, unique man who is perfect and different from all other men.

When It Looks Like Love, but It Really Isn't

Does Love Between Men and Women Really Exist?

The question that haunts most people, particularly after relationship disappointment and disillusion, is whether love really exists. When intimate relationships between men and women break apart with an explosion of raging negatives and overwhelming confusion, sadness, and helplessness, can we assume that what had been experienced before was love?

Looking beyond the philosophical abstractions and intellectualizations, an examination of the process dynamics that exist between men and women can illuminate this age-old question. Can love between men and women really exist, when:

- Men and women have a different experience of personal reality. What he sees as closeness is different from what she sees as closeness.
- Men are externalized, while women are internalized. Their direct energy and involvement in the personal is very different. Women typically feel they give more in a relationship and they resent it.
- The process is not balanced, creating distortions in experience. Because men *act* and women *react*, women feel controlled and angry, while men feel responsible and guilty.
- Men can rarely communicate their inner experience honestly without alienating women. Men have to hide their true selves and feelings in order to sustain the relationship.
- So long as blame and guilt exist, love is tenuous at best.
- Very few couples can negotiate conflict fairly, can

express their negative feelings safely, or can express anger clearly without alienating each other. Can love exist when these critical components of authentic caring are absent?

- What men and women intend and how their intentions are experienced by the other partner, especially in critical areas, are different. What men do to express love to women is not received that way, and what men believe is funny often is experienced by women as hostile. Similarly, what women experience as expressing legitimate needs, men tend to experience as pressure or smothering.

- Many relationships have as their starting point an object-to-object basis (i.e., her physical appearance and his vocation and money-earning ability).

- Few relationships begin without romance, which involves the temporary denial of resistance and conflict and the inflation of the other person as someone unique.

- Gender needs tend to be bottomless and non-negotiable, which causes anger toward the other partner who is seen as being unwilling to fulfill those needs.

The word "love" is an abstraction, supposedly something that is or isn't there. The search for it initially motivates, then tortures ,many people who pursue it as something that exists in the lives of the "lucky ones" who "found it," have "hung onto it," and are able to "make it grow." This unfortunate and primitive characterization of love that is deeply embedded in people from an early age blocks a meaningful understanding of the psychological complexity of this longed-for phenomenon.

Particularly between genders, love is a destructive and unfortunate mirage in the way that it prevents people who have come to believe that it somehow should just be there from having a functional relationship focus. For either partner to acknowledge their doubts about having that feeling when questioned by their partner derails individuals from bringing the experience and limits of the bond between a man and a woman into meaningful focus.

A more helpful approach would be to identify the components of a caring relationship, such as trust, attraction, relaxation in the other's presence, openness, balance of power, and the existence of a healthy experience of closeness and distance, to determine whether they exist. Once the word "love" becomes the main concern, it tends to end the conversation to the extent that one is asked to disclose whether it is or is not present. The tendency is to proclaim its existence falsely and then flee from further discussion. Once it is determined that the feeling of "love" supposedly does not exist many believe they are living a lie, even when in fact they acknowledge that they've never truly felt it before and only believe it exists based on the perception of couples one does not know well.

The fact that "love" can't really exist between traditional men and women who have polarized experiences of the relationship is not a negative statement, but rather a directional or guidepost to make sense of what actually keeps two people from having a closeness based on knowing and interacting with the full reality of the other.

When Traditional Women Fall in Love

Men's egos—and their need to believe the unbelievable—cause them to perceive a woman's love as pure and selfless, unadulterated by the "base" motives men have. Partly because acting selfless is a byproduct of feminine socialization, men interpret love by her as being of, by, and for itself and somehow deeper than their own.

Men confuse sexual attraction and fixation for love, while women confuse their desire to be rescued and taken care of for love. Women believe they love more than men because their need is to fuse and lose themselves in the relationship significantly more than their partners.

Fairy tales about Cinderella and Sleeping Beauty teach us that for women, falling in love has to do with being rescued

- from their dysfunctional family

- from their low self-esteem
- from a dire economic situation
- from an abusive relationship
- from the need to feel validated as a woman.

When women "fall in love" with a rescue object, it has no more to do with the man as a person than when men fell in love with a woman as a sex object. Once women get what they want and need, namely being rescued, they lose interest and motivation and the negative elements of the man begin to come into focus.

When women fall romantically in love in order to be rescued, their use of the man as an object is in denial, and when they begin to find fault in him, they blame it on the man, when in fact he has not changed from the person they formerly adored. She chose to see him through distorted love eyes initially when she needed him, much as men do when they desire a woman sexually and have not yet had her.

Men often feel disappointed and betrayed when a woman who had them on a pedestal begins to find endless faults. "I thought she really loved me," he thinks to himself. Disappointment and criticism on the woman's part grows to rage until finally all that is left of the original romantic feeling is her revulsion at the man's process:

- He's impossible to get close to and hard to read.
- He's a control freak.
- He's self-centered.
- He's cold.
- He's angry.
- He's afraid of closeness.
- He's always thinking about something else.

Once again, a man's defensive need to believe the unbelievable, namely that a woman can just meet him and magically "fall in love" with him because she somehow has managed to see him as he wants and needs to be seen, is the real cause of most men's resistance to and cynicism about love and marriage. When a traditional woman romantically falls in love, it is based on deeper defensive needs that she believes the man that she has just met can fulfill. The more easily such love arises, the greater the certainty that it will fade and transform into something else.

Is it Intimacy or is it Exploitation? How to Differentiate the Two

Women are sensitive to the experience of being viewed as an object and used by a man for sex, ego validation, or simply to fill the empty personal spaces of his life. Unless they have an equivalent agenda and design to use him in return, most women will sense the objectification and recoil from it.

What men still don't know is that because they are externalized and not tuned in to personal cues, they equally are vulnerable to being used, all the while believing it is love. Adding insult to injury, at the point where they have a gut-level reaction to the reality of being used that they sense—namely, that the connection is false and even dangerous—and begin to withdraw energy and involvement, they are liable to be accused of fearing closeness and commitment.

The guilt and self-hate that lurks just below the surface when men relate intimately may cause them to believe this accusation and take it seriously, and believe their resistance is a symptom of being dysfunctional. Once that happens, a crazy-making downward spiral has been launched; it will be hard for him to distinguish real from unreal, what he senses and feels coming from her versus the effect of his own problem areas.

Initially, it is simple for men to distinguish an exploitive agenda from genuine interest, attraction, and love. When exploitation is the motive and the exploiter senses she will not get what she wants or needs, she loses interest immediately and withdraws emotionally or becomes hostile and blaming. When care, connection, attraction, and love are real—meaning they have to do with the man as a person and not as an object to be used—the bond is not fragile and is not readily broken. The woman will not threaten to abandon her partner just because her desires are thwarted.

For a man to distinguish how often his experience of love and caring with a woman in the past has been real, he need only reflect on whether the woman continued to maintain interest, contact, concern, and love once she determined that her agenda was not going to be met. If the ending was abrupt and terminal, then he was not a person to her, but an object. Like an object, he is discarded once he was found to be useless.

No matter how romantic they seem, relationships with women that hang by a thread called "give me what I want or I'm gone" are best terminated early on, because the end is already built into the beginning. That is, as a stepping stone for her needs, he will be pushed aside once she has succeeded in getting what she wanted.

A man who is being used is an unknowing victim of sexism. *Sexism* is the unconscious transformation and use of the opposite sex as an object for one's own needs, gratification, and tension-reduction as opposed to intrinsically relating to the other as a person. Those who objectify or use others are usually in denial of their motives. They believe and will vehemently defend their belief that they are not using, but really loving and relating.

Romance tends to obscure the real nature of the interaction, but a man can sense when he's being used because he is afraid to be himself, to say what he thinks, and to show himself as he would ordinarily for fear that he will disappoint and antagonize his partner, and be rejected.

The man who flaunts his symbols of material success or his career potential, like the woman who flaunts her physical appearance and sexuality, is inviting being used and is colluding with that tendency in his partner, although he will deny that and will assert that he is just trying to make himself attractive.

Being Used: The Indicators

When a man is being used, most of the relationship interaction revolves around his function as a man, such as spending money, talking about commitment, or making future plans about marriage. When these interactions are not in the forefront, the energy between him and his partner wanes or dies. He senses correctly, that if he were not able to perform the functions that make him attractive (i.e., if he lost his job or ran out of money) that he would lose the love of his partner.

When a man is being used, he feels best and his partner seems happiest and most loving toward him when he is doing for her. When he is not doing for her, there is little energy between them.

A man can identify when he is being used when conversations very early on in the relationship turn to commitment and he has a sense that there is a relentless underlying pressure to move in that direction or his partner will leave. That is, when he is being used, the commitment is more important than the relationship to her: If he wavers or it becomes clear that commitment is something he is not ready for, she will lose interest, end the relationship, withdraw sexually, or lose her motivation ever to speak to him again.

From the beginning, when a woman's main interest in and attraction to a man is based on "What does he do?" he has already been objectified. Though initially he may be proud of what he does, and pleased that she appreciates it, ultimately his feelings will be the same as a woman who draws a man's attention because she's beautiful and then becomes resentful and insecure if she feels that her physical attractiveness is the primary basis of the relationship for him.

Particularly in these troublesome times, it is no longer a luxury to allow oneself to overlook the difference between a relationship that is based on genuine liking and caring versus a relationship founded on objectification and exploitation. The latter has the characteristics of being intensely romantic and exciting at its inception, and horrific and destructive as it reaches its inevitable endpoint, falling under the weight of objectification, rather than attraction based on authentic caring.

Are Men Women's Clients?
Women know men as men know their clients and the customers who they depend on for their livelihoods. If a woman avoids or rejects a man, it is not simply because of his lack of attractiveness, but because she believes or can see that she will not get what she needs from him. This is much like a man who will not continue relating to a client when he sees he will not succeed in closing a deal.

Women who relate to men out of their security needs know men much better than men know women, because men do not view women as critical to their future lifestyle and survival. Just as employees know the employer far better than vice versa, women know men far better than men know women.

Women who are successful with men are like men who are successful in the business world. They read their customers clearly and know how to manipulate them and "close the deal," even when they are in denial of what they are doing. It feels like love to her at the time, just as a man believes that he really likes and cares for his best customer when the deal is being closed.

Women know how to make a man feel good about himself so that she can get what she wants from him, just as a man knows how to make his customers and clients feel good about themselves, so he can get their business.

Women fall in love with objectively unattractive men if those men meet their needs. They reject other men who may be objectively far more attractive but where there is no prospect of getting what they need.

Women generally are in denial of their manipulation of men, and will insist that they really care about and actually like them, just as men tend to be in denial of their opportunism and manipulation of clients, and will say they really care about and actually like them.

The woman who is adept at getting what she wants from men does so as invisibly and subtly as men do who are skilled at getting what they want in the world of business. The better they are at it, the more impossible it is to see them at work.

What men still don't know is that a woman's love, when it is founded this way, will be fragile and volatile, and based primarily on the level of her inner security rather than on her caring for him as a person.

Why Women Are Also Incapable of Intimacy

It is generally assumed that men are damaged in their capacity for closeness and intimacy. If intimacy is defined as a loving closeness with another person, then it is usually true that the early conditioning of men to be performers and competitors in the impersonal competitive world limits their intimacy capacity. Women are assumed to have a greater capacity for intimacy than men because they express caring emotions and allow themselves to be dependent and close in relationships more easily. Yet, a closer look will provide a different perspective.

True intimacy is love and closeness based on knowledge of the inner reality and inner experience of the other. However, in romantic relationships, closeness ends or is put into crisis when men describe honestly their inner experiences to women. Women assail the relationship behavior of men and men acknowledge what they are told. Rarely is the opposite true. Men accept the reality of women more than women accept the reality of men.

The fact that a woman's priority is placed on personal needs bears no relationship to a genuine capacity for intimacy. To be loved and known, and to be fully comfortable expressing one's personal self, are two major components of intimacy. There are few men who have received that from a woman. The opposite holds true. A woman's love for a man is contingent on his participating in her romantic fantasy of what he and the relationship should be. Few men risk challenging or undermining that fantasy. Instead, they play by the rules of romance even when it feels uncomfortable, knowing that being loved by her is fragile and easily broken once he reveals his resistances and unromantic feelings.

When it Looks Like Love: How Gender Process Distorts Relationship Perception

What men still don't know is that feminine accommodation feels like love, but it isn't. It is defensive and a denial of a woman's boundaries caused by the anxious need to be pleasing and attractive to him. The fallout for the man is her feeling of being controlled and not having an identity, the cause of which she will attribute to him.

Feminine fusion craving feels romantic and loving, but it isn't. Rather, it is defensive and a flight from her separate self and represents her need to be rescued and to lose herself in a relationship. Fusion craving transforms into the anxiety-driven, bottomless need for reassurance and closeness.

Feminine repression of aggression and her compulsive niceness feels like caring, but it is not. It's a defense against and a denial of anger and conflict. The fallout or result is the buildup of anger that is repressed and that places pressure on the male, who is seen as the not-nice damager of the relationship. Along the way, there is her catastrophic overreaction to his anger and expression of conflict in the form of tears and fear that reinforce his guilt, sense of failure, and self-hate.

Her intense focus on the relationship feels like love, but it isn't. It is an out-of-balance obsessiveness that erodes her ability to deal effectively with external matters. Therefore, she seeks protection, and if she doesn't get it, she falls out of love.

Her romantic way feels like love, but it isn't. Romance is her way to get intense needs met and to overcome her deeper resistance to the reality of closeness with a man. She romanticizes him and the relationship to make it larger than life and to make the man seem as though he is different from other men and therefore palatable enough so that her powerful needs can be met. Later, her romantic feelings will turn to rage when she is disappointed and frustrated that he's not who she initially believed him to be. In the end, she will probably decide that he is just like every other man.

Manipulation can feel like love, but it isn't. What women unconsciously do with men is what good business or professional men do in the business world. They project images, give the client what he wants, and act interested, warm, and caring in order to achieve a goal. When her goal is reached, the positives fade away and are replaced by indifference or even resentment.

"Needing you" feels like love, but it isn't. "Needing you" is anxiety-driven and the love only lasts as long as the needs last, and as long as she feels her partner can fulfill them. When the needs change, or she loses faith in his ability to fulfill them, love fades and disappears.

Her desire to be committed looks like love, but it isn't. Commitment reduces a woman's anxiety and discomfort that build when a relationship doesn't seem to be going anywhere. Commitment validates her value as a woman. If he resists commitment or can't meet its demands, he loses her love. Her love is contingent on the commitment that she seeks.

Men don't read personal cues well when those cues are less than totally overt. It's common for the man to believe that he is loved when something much different actually is happening. His blind spots are the basis for the panic and desperation that he feels when the woman's façade is lifted and the deeper truth is revealed, namely that there was so much that he really didn't know about love.

When The Relationship Environment Is Poisoned

A Portrait of the Toxic Relationship

What could be a crueler relationship irony and paradox than the fact that the traditional marriage of the perfect man/perfect woman, Mr. Football Hero and Ms. Gorgeous Cheerleader, is also the recipe for profoundly poisonous relationship chemistry?

What men still don't know is that the more they approximate the masculine ideal, and the more women approximate the feminine ideal, the more toxic they become to each other. Counterpart processes polarize and trigger the unhealthiest aspects of each, as he becomes the toxic man and she becomes the toxic woman. Here is the profile:

Him	Her
1. Ever-expanding ego: He can't listen, is full of himself, has answers to everything; and believes he's always right and other people are "stupid."	1. Dissolving ego: She doesn't know who she is or what she wants, has low self-esteem, feels she knows little, is easily intimidated or made to feel she's wrong, and believes she is a "nobody" and stupid.
2. Believes personal problems can be solved with logic and willpower, is critical of and impatient with emotional displays, and resists and resents conversations about relationships and personal matters.	2. Believes problems can be solved with love and compassion and by discussing them endlessly. She emotionalizes, says irrational things, and can't turn off her tirades or be reasonable.

3. He is readily distracted and bored, particularly by personal, intimate, or non–goal-oriented interactions.	3. She is readily pulled in by almost anything personal. She talks on and on and can't stop once she engages in a personal discussion.
4. He craves high levels of stimulation in order to get or stay involved. Otherwise he is easily bored and distracted.	4. She can easily "do nothing" and feel content (i.e., sit around, talk about "silly" things, "waste time," sleep endlessly).
5. "He is impossible" to get close to.	5. She gets close to anybody; she is always available for a hug or a new connection or friendship, or an intimate conversation.
6. He is only able to "do," not to "be." When he's not "doing," discomfort, anxiety, and resistance build rapidly.	6. She is able to "be" but has trouble "doing" in the direction of an impersonal goal. She gets mired in the present.
7. He is a non-toucher. Physical closeness with no reason makes him uncomfortable.	7. She craves physical, sensual contact, such as a hug, a kiss, a hand held, or a massage.
8. He is out of touch with his body, ignores pain signals, denies his fatigue, is contemptuous of dieting, and must perform at all costs, even when he's not well.	8. She is obsessively aware of her body and every change in it or pain message that it sends, aware of every ounce she gains or loses, what she eats, and how she feels. She fatigues easily.

9. He is prone to disconnection and oblivion facilitators such as alcohol, televised sports, work, computers, projects, and "working out."	9. She is prone to fusion (love / closeness / intimacy) substitutes such as food, romance, and soap operas, talking on the phone to friends and family, shopping, and spiritual or psychic beliefs and pursuits.
10. He is easily irritated or angered and substitutes hostility for vulnerability; he is cold and distant when he is hurting.	10. She can't get angry even when she's being abused or betrayed and she cries when she's been hurt or upset. She readily feels and acts the part of the victim.
11. His is a "my way or the highway" philosophy. He is distracted and uninterested when he is doing something he hasn't chosen to do; he makes instant decisions and defends them vociferously.	11. She obsesses about decisions and can barely make one. She has a hard time defining what she wants and worries about her decisions. She has trouble saying no, says yes, and then resists passively later.
12. He is completely lacking in personal self-awareness and denies his alienating impact.	12. She is always noticing and obsessing over things about herself: what she did wrong, what she's all about, etc.
13. He is incapable of personal empathy and views expressions of distress as weakness and stupidity. He can't grasp what others feel and experience and is readily and unknowingly hurtful.	13. She sympathizes and empathizes readily and often gets inappropriately over-involved. She gets manipulated, conned, and sidetracked by those who want to use her vulnerability against her.

14. He is cold and unemotional.	14. She is full of feelings and has exaggeratedly intense emotional responses.
15. He is incapable of playfulness since everything must have a purpose and a goal to motivate him.	15. She gets mired in the moment. She is easily distracted by "silly" activities and sidetracks.
16. He is compulsively competitive. He won't participate if he's sure to lose; winning is the motivation and losing hurts, distresses, and angers him.	16. She fears aggression and can't compete. She wants everybody to feel like a family.
17. As he gets older, he becomes increasingly walled off from personal involvement.	17. She has poor personal boundaries, so she melts into others and loses herself in many relationships.
18. He sexualizes relationships and tends to be obsessive about sex. It is the principal way that he relates to women.	18. She is fearful and resistant of sex. She readily pulls away and withholds sexually unless she has a reason or it is intimate and romantic.

The toxic male, on a personal level, is oblivious to the poisonous impact of his process because that very process may be the same one that facilitates his success, achievement, and competitive advantage in the outside world. Since he usually gets what he wants "out there," he believes that what he thinks and the ways that he is are the best ways to be. He is toxic because he is self-centered and closed, yet is convinced that he is loving, generous, and wonderful.

Likewise, the most appealing feminine process characteristics on a content level can be the most polarizing and damaging in impact on a process level. Specifically, the latter triggers the most self-destructive impulses in a man, which also occur invisibly on a content level (they fall into his process blind spots), so that he is unaware of what is triggering his defensive behaviors.

The polarization of the classic sought-after romantic relationship has a built-in, self-destructive potential that is neither partner's fault and that has nothing to do with trying or giving up, even though one or both will attempt to find a reason in the other's behavior to hang blame on. In doing so, one kills the potential for learning about one's own contribution to the toxic endpoint in order to work toward not repeating the polarization process.

Knowing When to Leave

When a relationship is fully poisoned, with a woman who sees herself as an abused victim and a man who has become stone cold, angry, depressed, and self-hating, it's time to leave. Without intense therapeutic intervention no change will occur and the toxic atmosphere can only worsen.

Women who see themselves as abused victims don't see their equal participation in the downward spiral. They think therapy is about getting the man to change and become more loving. Relationship change, however, is impossible without each partner seeing their separate contributions and working on them.

The more of the following that are present, the greater the certainty that for the sake and well being of both, it's time to say goodbye.

- One remark can cause an explosion whose effects go on for days or weeks.
- Eating out or going to the movies is almost the only form of interaction and recreation that can be done without tension and boredom.
- Personal discussions quickly reveal the vast difference in how the two see things. Irritation, misunderstandings, and a sense of hopelessness arise readily in discussions.

- The degree of distortion between what one says and what the other one hears can be shocking.
- Social invitations are all but dried up; there are frequent comments about the absence of friends and the need to call "so and so," but it doesn't happen.
- Much of the time she's depressed and exhausted, while he becomes an obsessed workaholic and irritable when pulled away from his focus.
- She escapes through eating and soap operas and magical, spiritual, or religious pursuits. He escapes through drinking, work, and sports on television.
- You sleep together, but without touching. You deliberately avoid physical contact in bed.
- Sex, when it happens, has no affectionate foreplay. It's a ritual act of tension release and not an interaction of closeness and love.
- When you're alone together fatigue and boredom set in quickly.
- The question, "Why don't you leave if you're so unhappy?" or fantasizing that the other person will get sick and die and that would be the easiest solution occurs regularly.
- Each imagines what it would be like to be alone or with another partner.
- The best discussions are about other people's tragedies and negative news events.
- You think that almost everybody has a better relationship than you do. You envy the closeness you see in others.

When a relationship is fully poisoned, it has lost its capacity for positive change or even non-combative conversation. Remaining in it in the hope and belief that it will improve by itself is a reflection of the fear of change and risk. Finally, it becomes a form of emotional and personal suicide.

Unraveling the Mysteries

When Women and Men Don't "Get It": Making Sense of Relationship Addiction

Why do women stay in relationships when they're clearly being treated in abusive ways? Why do men stay in relationships when it's obvious they're being made fools of? Why do women behave in provocative ways that they know from experience cause men to become angry or violent? Why do men allow themselves to be pushed and provoked in ways that will cause them to lose control? Why do women pressure men for commitment when it only causes men to close up and withdraw behind their walls? Why do men pressure and push a woman for sex when that's the last thing that will make her feel sexual? Why do these people repeat behaviors that get contrary results to what they believe they want, over and over again? In other words, why don't they "get it"?

The above describes manifestations of addictive relationship behavior. It looks and seems like love and passion, but on closer inspection, it's the same compulsive, out-of-control behavior we see in addictions.

What characterizes an addiction in a relationship and separates it from love? Foremost, it is behavior that doesn't make sense, and yet people do it, like a criminal coming back to the scene of a crime.

Second, like all addictions, the behaviors go rapidly into denial. The compulsive eater makes himself sick every time, vows never to do it again, but quickly forgets how sick it made him each time before.

Third, addictive behavior in relationships is controlled by tension and craving, with no ability to see the consequences and effects that will occur as a result.

Fourth, even addicted people know that doing what they do is crazy or irrational, and that their partners will always disappoint, manipulate, lie, or humiliate. They know it, but they still want to try it one more time in the irrational belief that somehow the next time things will be different. It's like believing that a person's DNA can change.

Relationship addictions are such that cherished values and other relationships don't seem of enough value in comparison and one is willing to give them all up. But for what? Essentially, for the right to destroy oneself, but to do it with the deluded self-righteousness of being a victim in love.

When Nice Guys Are Hated

Sam was a nice guy. He was reasonable, pleasant, supportive, and soft-spoken. In spite of these qualities, both his marriages ended with his wives hating him and out for blood. His first wife, though a professional woman herself, battled him through the courts over property and alimony, feeling she was entitled to almost everything as reparation. Sam, in turn, fought her through the courts to the tune of a legal bill in excess of $50,000.

His second wife was a shy and quiet woman 20 years his junior, who fell in love with him as his student, married him, and convinced him to adopt a baby. Three years later they divorced, and a vicious custody battle ensued because she was adamant that he should see the child as little as possible. This was Sam's only child and he wasn't going to be deprived of parenthood, so he went into debt battling her through the court and psychological evaluations.

Why did this soft-spoken, shy, intellectual man, who tried to be agreeable and caring, inspire such rage? The answer lies not in what he did, but who he was, namely his process, or what it was like for his partner to relate to him on an intimate level.

Sam was very much "the man" in his relationship process. Cut off from feelings, he related with intellectualisms and facts. He was obsessive in his belief and pursuit of detached, logical answers to every question. Heavily externalized, he lacked a sense of how he was experienced or who another person was, beyond their surface verbal interaction. Intellectually, he was competitive. This came across as criticism toward those who didn't appreciate his logic and knowledge. While he cared about people, women knew it was impossible to really get close to him. He was disconnected and detached.

He believed he had all the answers, which made him come across as arrogant and needing to be right. His disconnected intellectualism caused him to lack a sense of the other person's feelings. Sexually, he was always interested but in an impersonal way. That is, he was uncomfortable with kissing and touching. He was obsessive about his work and was always writing technical articles. When he related personally it felt mechanical, like relating to the computer he knew so well and wrote about.

Given these process elements, women who were initially attracted to him because of his intellectual achievements found him extremely frustrating on a personal level. He never seemed fully present. He turned every conversation into an intellectual discussion. He made his women feel stupid—because of his attitude, rather than by anything he actually did or said. After a while, women gave up on connecting with the inner person of Sam. The more they pursued it, the more he withdrew. So in the end, his best efforts at loving came to naught. Without a clue as to why—because he believed he really tried to be nice, reasonable, supportive and caring—women's frustration and rage toward him grew until they had to leave, and they left him without any sense of attachment or warmth, only with anger and a feeling that he was personally impossible, which was true.

What men still don't know about relationships is that disconnected and externalized process cannot remain camouflaged behind "nice guy" gestures and behaviors. In fact, because "nice guy" behaviors initially stoke women's fantasies of having found a "different and special" kind of man, the negative reaction and rage that occur once she begins to experience his underlying distancing process and realizes that he is just like other men will be greater than had he made no efforts at all to be "nice," because she will come to feel that she's been deceived.

Hopeless Pursuits: Futile Relationship Efforts by Men

What men still don't know is that in the end, they will fail at doing the things that most traditional men still attempt.

A man will try to explain himself in order to change a woman's mind as to what she feels. If he persists in trying, she will only become more convinced that he is completely incapable of hearing and understanding what she is saying.

A man will try to convince a woman that his attempt to help her wasn't patronizing or a kind of "put down." His intention may have been of the highest order, but as always, the road to his relationship hell will be paved with these kinds of "good intentions" that women experience as an offensive display of male chauvinism, or as she experiences it, "treating her like a child."

A man will try to satisfy a woman's need for closeness. The more he tries the more she will be convinced that he can't.

A man will try to convince a woman that the relationship is his priority if she believes it isn't. This falls into the blind spot that men have of believing that his intentions will be received by her in the way that he experiences them. If it doesn't feel that way to her, nothing a man says to prove otherwise will make a difference.

A man will try to convince a woman that he really isn't trying to avoid closeness with her. Closeness is a feeling, not an idea. If a woman feels a man is distancing her, any attempt to convince her otherwise will only convince her even more that she is right.

A man will try to prove to a woman that he's not afraid of intimacy. That fear is something women can see in a man, but not something that he can acknowledge in himself.

A man will try to use logic to talk a woman out of her feelings. Feelings are on a different plane than logic. Just as feelings can't refute logic, logic can't refute feelings.

A man will try to convince a woman that he's not a sexist if she thinks he is. Few, if any, can view their own sexism or their objectification of the opposite gender.

A man will try to show a woman that every bit of his success had to be fought for and will not remain without vigilance, continued focus, and hard work. Most women believe men are driven by their competitive needs and couldn't stop pursuing success even if they wanted or really tried to.

A man will try to convince a woman that she doesn't always know what's best for the children. Few women believe that a man knows how to parent, or can do it better than a woman. The attempt to do so would feel to her like a criticism, rather than a contribution.

A man will try to prove to a woman that men are different from what she believes they are. Her ideas about men have deep roots and a long history of buildup. They are not really open to factual discussion.

A man will seek appreciation or gratitude for having rescued a woman from a messy life situation. Women sense correctly that when men act as a rescuer, it is as much in the service of the man's ego as it is for her benefit.

A man will try to raise a woman's self-esteem by being supportive in order to make her feel good about herself. A woman's sense of her own worth or value comes from her process (how she relates), her sense of control and power, and from her history. Supportive comments or acts by a man cannot touch that.

A man will try to convince a woman that she already has enough clothing, that she looks good without makeup, that she doesn't need to lose weight, that she's competent and that her fears about the world are not rational, and that she can do it successfully herself. Trying to convince her of these things is comparable to a woman trying to convince a man that he has enough money, that he is unduly distrustful regarding others and the future, and that it is okay for him to lose or fail.

In general, hopeless pursuits are about a man's attempts to alter a woman's experience of herself and her life. Efforts to do so will not only fail, but will anger her as well because she will experience those attempts as discounting, diminishing, and not really understanding her.

The Abused Male

Emotional abuse, like everything in the male-female relationship when viewed from the perspective of process and polarized gender defenses, cuts both ways. It is acted out differently, but is equal in its damaging and destructive power. This notion that men can be equally abused, though in different ways, falls into the blind spot of believing that the woman, regardless of what she says or does, is right and the man is the jerk/perpetrator. It follows the stereotype that women are the carriers of love and that men are the spoilers of relationships. Both notions are so powerful in their psychological seductiveness that they are hard to see through. Furthermore, what makes abuse difficult to identify is that, for the person being abused, it often doesn't feel like abuse. This is probably more so for men than for women in relationships. Men are socialized to feel that they are responsible when things go wrong or badly, even when there is distortion on the woman's part in accusing a man of having been hurtful, rejecting, unsupportive, and distancing. Most often, he has little, if any, idea what she means or what he has actually done to warrant the accusations. Because his role in the relationship is to feel guilty and assume that he is the hurtful, damaged one who can't love, or that he isn't as involved emotionally as she, he thinks he must be at fault.

The man most vulnerable to being abused in the traditional relationship, paradoxically, is the man who is the most dependent, plays the "nice guy" role, and tries the hardest. This is analogous to the female abuse victim who tends to be the "nice" accommodator, but with low self-esteem, who is continually looking for reassurance of love, has weak boundaries, and is deeply dependent.

With abused men, there is the added twist that to be loved in the traditional sense, men are supposed to exude confidence and dominance. The "nice guy" male partner who is abused does not, and so on a deeper level he repulses and frightens his woman partner because his weak behavior does not allow for the kind of balance and safety that she is accustomed to. At least part of her doesn't want the power that he gives her. It robs her of the romantic sense that she is being protected and cared for.

Externalized men use their aggression and control to intimidate, terrorize, and therefore victimize their overly dependent, fearful, reassurance-craving, low self-esteem partner. Because his abusive behavior is overt, it is easy to identify and label. At the same time, the way she colludes with, provokes, and facilitates his abusive behavior is difficult for all but the trained eye to see.

Abuse in committed relationships is almost always a two-way street. It is the product of a dynamic in which the perpetrator is facilitated, provoked, and polarized by his victim, who is often quite strong and capable of preventing these episodes but, for complex emotional reasons, does not. Women, as well as men, go on for years in relationships in which they are being hurt, cheated on, and lied to but they don't see it and they don't "get it" because it doesn't *feel* bad enough and because they rationalize and deny what is going on.

The male partner/husband is abused by the woman who uses various forms of manipulation of the man's guilt through aggressive blaming to fuel his self-hatred, feelings of responsibility, and sense of guilt. So he finds himself apologizing, and the more he does, the more punitive, cold, and rejecting she becomes. Meanwhile, his anxiety, self-hatred, and fear of abandonment increase, while his self-esteem plummets. Like the abused female, he may believe he is happy in the relationship, that he is loved and that if he could only be a little more sensitive and like she wants him to be, then everything would be all right.

Specifically, in the abused male partner syndrome, the guilt-ridden male finds himself apologizing and attempting to undo and mollify his partner for things that he is accused of doing but never actually did. He is responding to her negative interpretation because his guilt and anxiety over possible abandonment cause him to believe he might have done it. Perhaps he is told that a comment he made was hostile or sarcastic, or that the tone of his voice had anger or rejection in it. His reaction is "I didn't do that," or "I didn't mean it that way." But she is already using her interpretation to justify punishing and abusing him.

On a vacation together that he might have gone out of his way to plan at great expense, he may find the trip poisoned because she exaggeratedly responded to something he said or did, or didn't say or didn't do, but when he attempts to discuss the matter and explain himself, she will not or cannot hear it.

In all abuse dynamics, with either male or female victims, victims find themselves explaining and apologizing. For the man, it is his low self-esteem and giving away of power that causes him to explain himself, trying to convince his partner that he was not doing or meaning something the way she thought. To further reinforce his victim role, he is grateful and appreciative if she momentarily forgives him or even listens to him without further accusing or magnifying his behavior.

He is emotionally bullied into being on the defensive instead of simply stating, "I don't know what you're saying. If you really believe what you're telling me, then I believe you have a very distorted interpretation of me and you're going to have to acknowledge that and work on it, or our relationship will not survive." Instead, the abused male plaintively whines, "What did I do? I really didn't do that. And if I did, I'm sorry. I didn't mean it." When he gets a cold, rejecting response, he keeps on pursuing reassurance instead of withdrawing. "Do you still love me?" he asks pathetically. He is relieved if she feebly answers, "Yes," or panics if she doesn't.

By explaining himself and allowing her to get away with her distortions, he further reinforces his victim position. Instead of making things better, his explanations are ignored and seem to make things worse.

In other variations of the abused male syndrome, the "nice guy" male makes a spontaneous comment, humorous remark, or playful (and to his mind, affectionate) gesture. To his shock and disbelief, his partner reacts with rage and an accusing, blaming, attacking response that he doesn't understand but may apologize for ("If I sounded sarcastic, I didn't really mean to").

He might be accused and made to feel guilty for spending time with friends, deliberately ignoring her at a social event, working late, visiting children from a previous marriage, being too nice to an ex-spouse or coming home late. He knows in his heart that her interpretation of him is distorted, but he feels that maybe she's right, "I'm guilty."

Trying to respond to or answer her accusation, which he would not do had he maintained a sense of self-esteem and refused to answer distorted accusations, he may encounter a relentless harangue, a physically violent assault, or a diatribe that seems to have no end. Even when he tries to pull back, he may find himself pursued.

There are other forms of abuse of the male that are not recognized as such. These include manipulating him to get something material from him, flirtatiousness with other men in front of him, a passive-aggressive style that forces him to take responsibility for everything, an undermining of social plans at the last minute with self-centered and raging threats ("You can go to your damn boring boss's party alone!"), disparaging remarks made in front of other people about his skills as a provider or lover, and certainly the undermining of his relationship to his own children by presenting them with an ugly portrayal of him and his motives.

Just as women are often in denial of abuse, a man may not know or recognize that he is abused. He accepts negative interpretations, outbursts, accusations, and assaults because of his guilt and dependency, his fear of rejection, or his need to be a nice guy. However, the effect on him in terms of depression, self-hate, and the eventual destruction of his personal and maybe even work life, are every bit as damaging for him as for the battered wife.

4 *What Men Still Don't Know About Sex*

✓ *Do Women Really Like Sex?*

✓ *When He's Thinking about Sex, She's Thinking about Rescue*

✓ *Sexual Dysfunction as Truth Teller*

Do Women Really Like Sex?

On the face of it, women today seem more sexually liberated that their grandmothers were. Is this real or is it an illusion or mirage?

When women share early memories of sexuality, it's almost always negative. Women hear almost exclusively negative information about men and sexuality from the time they are little girls. As young girls and women, females are supposed to downplay their sexuality. Under anything less than ideal romantic conditions, most women can do without sex with a man indefinitely.

When looking at an attractive woman, most men primarily think of sex. Almost every date has the background noise of pressure from a man to move toward sex. Despite this ever present specter of sex, very few men, without considerable experience, personal therapy, and education about women's bodies, can be satisfying lovers. In fact, the mainstream man is, for most women, an inadequate lover.

Women tend to experience their sexuality not as a path to pleasure, but as a path to power and control over the man. Most women who go without sex for long periods of time don't really miss it. In fact, the longer they do without it, the more they insist it has to be under certain conditions or they would rather not participate. Even when women are in love, if they are angry or hurt, they back away from sex.

Indeed, where is there any solid basis for women to build and enjoy their sexuality with a man? It is no wonder that women so readily feel sexually harassed, or abused by men, even when men are doing nothing more than "acting naturally" and being themselves.

In few areas is the potential for breakdown between the genders more extreme and in few areas are the consequences for men misinterpreting and "not getting" the experiential reality of women more dangerous. Asking her how she feels about sex is not enough. Knowing the existence of the polarization and her early conditioning is crucial and never to be denied.

When He's Thinking About Sex, She's Thinking About Rescue

Women are continually disappointed, hurt, and embittered when they misread a man's sexual passion and advances as meaning that he's interested in them and in having a loving relationship. It is an *error of projection*, which is the tendency to believe that the opposite gender experiences things the way that you do. In extreme cases, the distortion produces the fatal attraction error and tragedy. He says to her, "You really excite me. I'm married, but I'd love to make love passionately just for the pleasure of it. No strings attached." She hears the words, but in her gut, if she's also attracted and interested, she doesn't really believe he means it that way. Instead, she feels that if he's *that* excited and passionate about making love with her, that he's unhappily married (probably true), and that he must really want to be with her but is reluctant to acknowledge it, and that after a time, he'll come around with the true feeling, which is that he really wants to be with her (probably not true). She believes it because this would be true for her.

When it finally sinks in that she's been used, there is a mixture of disappointment, hurt, and rage, and she wants revenge because she has become addicted to the intensity of his passion and involvement, which excites her and connects her to him. She wants it to continue the way that she believes it is or could be and can't grasp the reality.

Similarly, men are aware of their own manipulations but have a blind spot when it comes to reading or understanding a woman's motive and reality. When she comes on strong sexually, he thinks, "She must find me irresistible. She's really turned on to me sexually." Later, it may become clear to her that she doesn't want him as her fantasy man to rescue her, take care of her, and validate her. Often he is bewildered when the next time he calls she doesn't have the slightest desire to have sex with him. He is in disbelief. Somewhere deep inside he believes that she must really be longing for his body.

When men have an agenda that involves sexual fantasies and a woman responds positively, that woman also will have an agenda, but it's rarely the same as his. A man's initial agenda is almost always anchored in sexual interest. A woman's agenda, however, is anchored in fantasies of commitment, rescue, being taken care of, and being provided for. Women rarely have sex without an agenda for a committed relationship, just as men rarely try to have a relationship if they don't have an agenda that involves sex. Few men passionately pursue a woman when the motivation is just good conversation, companionship, or closeness.

Men's error of projection is to believe that women are being seduced and excited sexually by the wondrous sexual magnetism of the man and that she is not maneuvering to gain her agenda, just as he is. The man is disappointed and angered later, when the woman's real motives surface. At this point, some men will feel that they have been had. Women, probably even more so than men, need a powerful motive in order to get interested in a sexual relationship because their resistance, fear, distrust, wariness, and anger toward men are so great.

Sexual Dysfunction as Truth Teller

Men view their sexual response mechanically, as if it wasn't a direct expression of who they really are as people. What men still don't know is that in doing so, they lose important information about how they really feel in a relationship in their defensive quest to validate themselves as men. Also, they lose an important opportunity to see themselves more clearly.

Only men who objectify women think of their own sexual response in terms of performance, such as potency and impotence. Impotence implies performance standards, and further implies that a man's sexual response exists separately from his process, his feelings, his sensibilities, the relationship he is in, the conflicts in the relationship, and the conscious as well as unconscious feelings of his woman partner that affect the way he will respond to her sexually.

The traditional man unknowingly has sex in a disconnected way. The woman is an object, and his performance is related only to *his* tensions and need. Any vagina will do. For such men, labels of sexual dysfunction such as premature ejaculation and impotence are relevant because he is a machine, his penis is mechanical plumbing, and she is an object for his tension release. For the man who is evolving toward non-defensive personhood, the sexual response is a personal one that reflects and teaches him who he is, what he experiences, who she is, what the relationship is all about, and how it feels to him to be with her.

There are two basic components that are the ingredients of optimal sex: trust and attraction. When both exist, the body relaxes and responds to its maximum capacity. When one's personal self senses danger, or there is a lack of attraction, the body will resist or not respond at all, even if he thinks that he wants to.

When there are agendas, hidden or overt, such as a woman who is using her sexuality manipulatively for control, or who has a buildup of anger and rage that she denies and covers with an accommodating façade, the penis "knows" and responds with tension, fear, resistance, or withdrawal. The responses could be labeled with a diagnosis of medical dysfunction—but to the man's detriment, because he loses connection with the meaning of his response and what his deeper self is saying. In addition, men bring their process to bed and a man's need to control, his basic interest in or resentment toward his partner, or even his fear of rejection and failure can all translate into sexual dysfunction.

The combination of and interaction between women's and men's denied and blocked feelings and motives are manifested in bed. This can create sexual chaos and confusion over what one wants to believe or feel, versus what the deeper reality of the relationship really is. A man's defensive ego and need to perform transforms a potentially liberating and clarifying sexual response and resistance in him into a threatening one that he will seek to deny and overcome.

In light of the intense anger and fear that many women harbor toward men, and the manipulative way women learn to relate to men, the aware man will experience various degrees of sexual hesitancies and resistances. His masculine compulsion to perform will cause him to reject and seek to overcome his deeper survival response, to his detriment and torment.

5 What Men Still Don't Know About Women's and Men's Liberation

✓ HER
  » *Why A Promising Dream for Her Became a Nightmare for Him*
  » *Liberated Women: The Façade and the Reality*
  » *Understanding Accusations of Sexual Harassment*

✓ HIM
  » *Why Being the Sensitive Man doesn't Work*
  » *A New Age Myth for the Liberated Man*
  » *When Men Blame*

Her

Why a Promising Dream for Her Became a Nightmare for Him

Men's dream of women's liberation was that women would become partners with equal responsibility, where issues and differences could be discussed fairly, and men and women could maintain their separate identities and share equally in parenting and financial responsibility.

Instead, what men have experienced more often than not is the worst of both worlds. Specifically, women want to be free of traditional roles and responsibilities, but still romanced by a man who is stronger then they are and who is a protective rescuer. The reasons for that development are many.

- Feminism was an extension and defensive endpoint of traditional femininity, not a departure from it.
- Feminism was the end manifestation of blaming rage and a victim mentality, the interpretation of a traditional woman's experience. There was little discussion about how women had contributed to creating the problems they had with men and how they had invited and benefited from the same behaviors they were raging against. Feminism was born of victim energy with the guilt placed solely on the male.
- The burden of change was placed on men. Men were the sexists, the oppressors, and the pigs. There was no discussion of how women objectified men by using them as success and provider objects and the way that women expected and even demanded from men the very behaviors that they now protest.

- There was little exploration of the dynamics of femininity that cause women to be reactors rather than actors, and the way that dynamic sets into motion the process that results in women feeling controlled and inferior to men.
- There was no acknowledgment of women's part in maintaining the glass ceiling phenomenon, namely, the discomfort and resistance women experience when placing a priority on work and careers, nor the tendency of women to drop the ball on their ambitions when a desired relationship or the birth of a child pulled at them, nor the anger most women feel when they have a baby and the man is not supportive of their quitting their jobs to stay at home.

The liberated woman is a crazy-making disappointment for men because her changes and transformations involve attitude and ideology but not her deeper feminine process. Thus, she has traditional longings and needs, is attracted to men who are winners and reviles weaker or less ambitious men, and wants men to pay and lead unless she decides otherwise. For the man, there's a confusing sense that whatever he does, he stands to be wrong and blamed. If he treats her as an equal, it doesn't feel romantic to her. If he treats her in traditional ways, he is considered a chauvinist and a sexist.

Instead of having an equal partner who is self-aware, responsible, and wants to know him as a person, feminism has produced a doubly defensive woman who is on guard about her rights, but insistent that men be romantic and "make her feel like a woman" by acting like a real man.

Liberated Women: The Façade and the Reality

While traditional, role-bound relationships have their built-in craziness and unmanageability due to the defensive aspects of feminine process, the relationship with a liberated woman contains the same craziness overlaid with a mass of ideologically based attitudes and politically correct responses. Men are often fooled into believing that the expressed verbalizations and pursuits of a liberated woman are the essence and reality of her. The unmanageable, wild ride of traditional relationships becomes much more extreme due to the layer of liberated attitudes that cover the still-traditional core.

What men still don't know about the liberated woman is that her traditional reactive feminine process still remains, but is now layered over by defensive anger over being controlled, abused, or diminished. He is still expected to be "a man" and yet expected to not "act like a man" at the same time.

The romantic craving in the liberated woman remains, but it is now overlaid by bursts of righteous rage over men's sexism, which is neither negotiable nor open to a resolution in which both people are able to listen to and hear each other. He is judged and sentenced simply because he is a man and therefore a sexist and assumed abuser of women.

Most men can't distinguish the difference between a genuinely liberated woman and the traditional woman in liberated garb because they assess women based on surface, external, and literal responses. To him, because she says and does liberated things, she must be liberated. When that does not turn out to be the case, he finds himself in an uglier, more painfully vengeful relationship than with an acknowledged traditional woman because the liberated woman has become a double-blamer. She blames men for controlling and frustrating her traditional needs, but also for being sexist and abusive according to feminist or liberated ideology.

At the point where her righteous rage emerges, she is impossible to negotiate with. She has planted her feet fully on the higher ground of the morally superior, maligned, and abused victim, which locks her into an unapproachable, nonnegotiable posture.

The initial attraction and seduction of the liberated woman is that a man can talk more freely, fairly, rationally, and directly with her. Yet on a process level, the opposite turns out to be true; she is rigidly locked into her perception of herself as abused and morally superior

Understanding Accusations of Sexual Harassment

Men's defensive sexuality, which causes their sexual interest and behavior to be disconnected from feelings of love and caring, readily leads to equally defensive reactions in women who are sensitive to and threatened by the potential for exploitation, objectification, and the frustration caused by being seduced into interactions where their need for intimate connection will be frustrated.

In this age of in-your-face confrontation, accusation, and litigation, men need to see clearly how they are being perceived and interpreted, rightly or wrongly, and need to understand why it is occurring. The key to understanding and avoiding a woman's seemingly irrational accusations of abuse and harassment is to focus on how she interprets reality and not on what the man intends or believes he did. The wrong way to respond is to try to convince her that her interpretations or accusations are inaccurate.

The simplest and quickest way to be safe from these charges is to always assume that a woman's response to a man will be defensive and nonnegotiable. In fact, a woman often does experience what seems to men to be benign and even well-intentioned comments, kidding, playfulness, or flirting as hostile and abusive behavior. In years past, women accommodated men's egos so their real reactions to men's behaviors didn't show. Today they feel empowered to express their true feelings and to release their rage at his "abusive behavior."

While most women do not respond to or experience men's responses negatively, most women have the potential to do so, much in the way that men have a potential to overreact to external business or life events in a paranoid way, and to see attack and danger where it does not exist, or exists only slightly.

Men who choose to justify or rationalize their behavior and impact when it comes to matters of sexual behavior, intended or otherwise, do so at their own peril. They will never be heard in the way that they would like. Never is the gap between a man's intention and his impact more clearly pronounced than when he sees his behavior in a certain way while the woman perceives it completely differently. The non-defensive and aware male will put his energy into hearing and understanding the why and how of his impact and learn from that, rather than trying to explain himself. Apart from those occasional times when the woman is simply maliciously lying, it is never useful for a man to try and make the woman understand his reality of the situation because in the final analysis, he will fail and only be seen as defensive and in denial.

Him

Why Being the Sensitive Man Doesn't Work

For several decades, many men have made efforts to become sensitive to women's feelings and needs. That meant being careful about avoiding sexist words or actions, learning to listen, learning not to respond as if women were lesser than they, learning not to objectify women as sex objects, learning not to be controlling or dismissive or critical, not minimizing women's concerns and needs, and being careful not to express themselves in abusive tones and words.

After years of working at being sensitive, men discovered that not only didn't it work in creating closeness, trust, and balanced, loving relationships, but many found they became the object of even greater anger. They were labeled as wimps, hypocrites, or weak, and incurred more blame than when they were insensitive and not trying.

What men still don't know is that being sensitive hasn't worked because it is a simplistic, one-sided solution to a complex, reciprocally polarizing dynamic. Efforts to be sensitive simply reinforced the myth and distorted belief that relationship problems were *his* fault. As long as women were not including their defensive process as an equal contributor to the relationship experience, and were not working equally to overcome their defensiveness, matters couldn't improve.

When men are being sensitive, without an equal commitment on the woman's part to acknowledge her process and how that impacts her partner, it affirms the distorted perception and belief that he is the spoiler, and her problems and responses are only the byproducts and consequence of how he treats her.

As long as her denied process and its impact are not acknowledged and changed, his being sensitive will be experienced as guilt-motivated weakness and powerlessness. Ultimately, this will repel, enrage, and threaten her, even though initially it may charm her. His being sensitive will be a threat to her traditional needs to be protected and taken care of.

Until and unless a woman acknowledges and works equally to transform her defensive process, a man is better off not trying to be sensitive. While she may still be dissatisfied, at least the devastating deeper rage and threat that a man's weakness triggers in her won't develop.

The solution for a woman who would like to make her partner more sensitive is not to focus on teaching a man to do so, but for her to learn to relate in a nontraditional process. As a person rather than as a feminine woman, she would seek to overcome her tendencies to

- blame
- feel victimized
- cry
- react rather than act
- resist being clear about what she wants
- look for protection, rescue, and safety
- expect a magical, ever growing romantic intimacy
- assume power passively and indirectly through manipulation, guilt-making, and acting as if she were weaker, more fragile and vulnerable than he
- use her sexuality as a reward and mechanism of control
- expect him to take the bulk of responsibility for decisions and finances
- deny her own immense power in the relationship because of his dependency on her for personal connection, validation as a lovable person, and sex
- not see the impact of her emotionalizing in promoting his closed off attitude.

A man's effort to be sensitive is a route to painful and out-of-control relationships unless it is met equally and in tandem with a woman's focus on her process and the ways that she polarizes and contributes equally to the relationship's problems. Once again, men need to recognize the gap between what they intend and how they are experienced. The man trying to be sensitive would be dismayed to discover that his attempts are not coming through in the way that he believes. To avoid the bitterness and resentment that he will come to feel when he sees his efforts at having been sensitive come to naught, which they usually will, he must once again focus on what the woman sees and what she does with that, rather than what he believes or intends. In the worst-case scenario, she may see his efforts as a form of wimpiness that she can exploit. In the best-case scenario, she may appreciate his trying, but be turned off by his ineptness or inauthenticity.

A New Age Myth for the Liberated Man

Once upon a time, there was a young man who loved a young woman. He did everything right, the way a man should, and it came out all wrong. He tried to be supportive, and she said he was being patronizing. He opened up about his pain, and she made him feel like a wimp. He let himself get close, and she said he had become too dependent. He showed her his feelings, and she got scared. He held back sexually because he didn't want her to think that was what he mainly wanted, and she lost respect for him and insulted his manhood. He refrained from making important decisions by himself that involved them both, and she said he was too wishy-washy. He never raised his voice or got angry, and she wondered about his manliness.

He went to his men's group and they told him he had lost her respect by not being a warrior-man, and by allowing her to shame him. They empowered him to be a real man again. He became decisive and she accused him of being controlling. He drew his boundaries and re-owned that which was his, and she said he was afraid to be vulnerable or to share. He "stopped taking crap" and told her to "back off" when she made him angry, and she said he scared and intimidated her. He started telling her exactly what he thought and felt, without apology or shame, and she said he was being abusive. He started to be more assertive sexually, and she got enraged and said he was acting like a pig. He became more detached instead of emotional, and she said he was like a machine with no feelings. He concentrated on his "mission" or work, and she complained that he was never there for her. Finally, she left him.

He became seriously ill, and his men's group sent him a "get well" card to empower him to get better. But they never came to visit. He never saw or heard from them again until he got better. When he was ready to return to the group, he really didn't feel like going. So they told him he was running away from his real feelings and was resisting growth.

When Men Blame

Many men feel ripped off by ex-wives, attorneys, the courts, and "the system." However, men's experience of being wounded has a positive side. It levels the playing field of gender warfare created by traditional male-female bonding rituals. These rage-producing experiences of feeling helpless, used, and abused make it possible for men to empathize with and to understand the victim mentality of women.

Potentially, men and women alike can know what it means to feel discriminated against and abused. In the best-case scenario, this could result in men and women becoming more understanding of, and sensitive to, each other's dilemmas and vulnerability. That could lead both genders to an awareness of the bigger picture and dynamic that brings even the most well-intentioned and caring couple to a similar place: one of feeling used, abused, and misunderstood by the other. Neither is consciously or intentionally doing that, but it occurs to both in spite of the best efforts and intentions of each partner.

In traditional relationships, there is an absence of a balanced and healthy foundation that makes genuine caring and communication possible. Men manage to gain and remain in relationships via external control and intimidation, while women enter into and remain in relationships using the mechanisms of romantic fantasy, accommodation, and manipulation.

This traditional process ensures that the relationship will become symptomatic and produce resentment and communication breakdowns as it moves steadily out of control. Once either partner feels sufficiently secure to do so, that partner will seek release from the frustration, pain, and anger of the relationship.

At the termination of the relationship, when either partner feels abused and betrayed by the other and gets stuck in that interpretation, while ignoring their own process contribution and its impact, it means they don't get it. No learning will take place that could produce an improved future relationship with a new partner.

Furthermore, when either men or women use the delusion of victimization to blame institutions, issues, and people, and to demand personal vindication, they are ignoring the blind spots, rigidities, distortions, and defensiveness of their own process that helped create their pain. They have lost the bigger picture and traded short-term vindication for long-term growth.

At the end of a traditional relationship, and the gender warfare it produces, it is all-too-easy to see the irrational victim rage of the other, but difficult to see one's own equal contribution. In freely chosen adult love relationships, there are no victims, only the seeming illusion of such.

As a psychotherapist looking beyond the surface or content issues of the hundreds of relationships in crisis that I have worked with, it is apparent that each partner participated equally in the deterioration of the relationship. Sometimes that contribution is by omission, such as a denial of reality, an inability to set boundaries or express anger or to acknowledge and negotiate conflict, or the excruciating impact of one's passivity and reactivity. The contributor by omission looks blameless.

Men who get stuck in their anger and are unable to see the toxic effect of their externalized process in the relationship breakdown vent rage against attorneys, courts, "the system," or women. They lose the golden opportunity of becoming aware of their own alienating, disconnecting impact that is their contribution to the rupture of relationships.

Men are as responsible for everything that happens to them in a personal relationship as women are, though often they can't see that, particularly when they lived up to the definition of a good husband and good father as defined by society. Men are responsible for their lack of awareness when it comes to recognizing that women have an agenda that results in the objectification of the male, similarly to men who objectify women based on their sexual attractiveness. Women's motives for commitment, security and being rescued cause them to use men while being in denial of doing that, just as men deny when they sexualize, objectify, and try to control women.

Men are responsible for suspending their own logic and reason, when they see women's anger and blame everywhere else, including in their own past failed relationships, and believe somehow that their latest romance will be an exception. They are responsible for denying their own confusion, fear, and powerlessness in the early phase of their relationships. They buy into the notion that women are fragile, and that a man is responsible for making or breaking a relationship solely by his actions.

When men blame, they are missing the point in exactly the same way as women when they blame, particularly in committed relationships where men and women are free to choose who they are with. The meaningful questions are, "What is it about me that caused me to be drawn to this person?" and, "In what way did I bring the things that hurt and anger me upon myself?" Anything short of that will only doom a man to repeat the same experience with his next partner until he finally gives up in bitterness and resentment and falsely concludes that all women and all relationships are the same.

6 What Men Still Don't Know About Their Family Experience

The Family Dance

The Dance of Family Dysfunction

Dysfunction is a built-in, inevitable consequence of the dynamic of traditional man-woman relationships. The outward picture differs from one family to the next but the underlying pain, conflict, frustration, and endpoints are similar.

Well-intentioned parents are blamed by their children and search for specific events they can identify as "the cause." This makes real, meaningful, and permanent change difficult, if not impossible, because the true source of the damage is not being identified. That is, the same dysfunctional dances and arguments are transferred from one generation to the next. Each generation believes that they can do better than the previous one. Instead it gets worse. When dysfunction travels through generations, redeeming features are progressively lost while stripped-down, blatant dysfunction remains.

The Steps of the Dance

- The disconnected man and the romantic, fusion-craving woman meet and fall in love. They marry.
- The closer she wants to get, the thicker his walls of disconnection become because he uses his energy for achieving, performing, and attaining the goal.
- Her frustration builds, and her neediness and anger build with it, causing him to enclose and disconnect even more.
- She turns to her children for the fulfillment of her intimacy or fusion needs.

- She fuses with her daughter, who becomes addicted to an intensity of enmeshment that becomes her standard for what she wants and needs in adult intimacy. In addition, she learns to have her mother's reactions and emotional responses of anger and pain toward her father.

- She fuses with her son, who becomes closer to her than to his dad. He is imprinted by her and at the core he identifies with her. This creates identity and gender confusion in him: "Am I a boy, like my dad says I better be, or am I a girl because I have my mother's feelings and reactions?" Fusion with mother causes him to resent and misunderstand his father the way his mother does.

- To control and deny his mother's imprint, the son develops a macho defense system. He protests and responds to the extreme to prove that he's really a man. He becomes a fully externalized, aggressive, compulsively sexual, cold, and distant person in order to wall off his confused inner self.

- The daughter becomes addicted to the kind of emotional and interpersonal intensity she had with mom. To get that, she romanticizes her relationship with a man so she can re-experience the intensity she equates with being close and loving, like mother.

- The man craves anchoring and love, but his defenses destroy his interpersonal sensitivities and capacity. So, he is pulled in by the woman's "magical" romantic ardor. She makes love seem easy and fun. He loves the validation, intensity, and attention, like he got from his mother. All he has to do is keep performing and achieving. She does the relationship work.

- Temporarily, he is no longer confused. She makes him feel like a man. Meanwhile, she feels rescued. She can have romance and be taken care of by a provider, decision-maker, and achiever.

- Because she's romantic and addicted to fusion, and he

seems to like it, she projects that he will be as romantic as she. However, he is only riding on her energy that will steadily dissipate and dissolve.

- They marry. His externalized self takes over. He starts doing, performing, achieving, and controlling. She feels depressed, angry, and disillusioned in response.
- They have kids. She turns away from him and toward her children for satisfaction.

The dysfunctional cycle continues to play itself out, but as the cycle continues from generation to generation it accelerates. Women and men who become progressively more incapable and fearful of relating to each other enter into increasingly stressful, dysfunctional relationships.

Why Women Change after Marriage

Often a man will complain that the woman he married is not the same as the woman he courted and initially fell in love with. Women seem to transform and become someone different after the wedding.

Do women actually change? In the deepest sense, they don't. However, in terms of the behaviors they show to men, yes. These are the reasons.

- She "got what she wanted" (like men after sex).
- She no longer needs to see him romantically (as being different from other men).
- There is a power shift that occurs when she no longer has to please him in order to hold onto him.
- Her accommodation to his process builds anger in her because of a sense of being controlled and of losing her identity.
- Men cannot satisfy women's needs for reassurance, closeness, and keeping things positive, but she can't see or believe that.
- When women stop trying, a relationship vacuum is created. He had been riding on her energy.

- Can a woman's caring last in the face of her fear, anger, reactivity, and resentment over what she isn't getting?

For men to avoid the nightmarish experience of witnessing the transformation of their partner into someone completely different once they have permanently committed to her, men need to take responsibility for the many blind spots created by their egos and by the relationship shortcomings generated by their masculine socialization. Both of these make it impossible for them to see that during courtship, the woman simply acted as a mirror and that what men had fallen in love with was not who the woman is, but how they believed she perceived them and the way that she related to them. Particularly during courtship women primarily react, accommodate, and deny conflict and negative emotion in order to achieve their goal of being in a committed relationship. Ultimately, it is men's need to falsely believe in their own wonderfulness and to avoid confronting their own relationship deficiencies and dysfunctions that cause them to be drawn in by a woman who is not showing who she really is, but is only reflecting back to the man the way he would like to believe that he is.

Women don't change after marriage; they only stop being the reflectors of a man's ego. A psychologically healthy male would never have been attracted to a woman in the first place who was primarily a reactor, pleaser, accommodator, and avoider of conflict. To that extent, the trauma of experiencing a woman morph into somebody else is something he brought upon himself, rather than something that she did to him.

Why Wouldn't a Married Man be Angry?

In their marital relationships, men are commonly viewed as angry. Though men tend not to process their personal experiences consciously, they may be responding to certain responses they receive in the family that leave them feeling blamed, unappreciated, and unloved in spite of their great efforts to be what the family needs. Some of the realities that weigh on them may help explain their irritability and angry demeanor.

Why Wouldn't a Man be Angry . . .

- when what he does for his wife and family become invisible and are not seen as acts of love and loving, and only what mom is and does is experienced as love and being loved.
- when what he does for a living is seen as his ego trip and is appreciated primarily in terms of the financial gains that allow others to buy more and better things that they eventually come to expect.
- when work is seen as having controllable limits, and success is something that just comes automatically. When he works long hours and comes home withdrawn and tense, he is seen as choosing work over family and having his priorities screwed up.
- when his concerns about finances, goal-setting, succeeding, and maintaining are experienced as negative, alienating, and pressure compared to mom's goals of love, closeness, feeling good, being happy, eating, enjoying oneself, and being "nice."
- when even his steadiness and best efforts, while mom is falling apart and acting hostile or crazy, still don't make the kids feel as close to him as they do to her.
- when his efforts to be helpful and honest are construed as critical and negative, while her input is seen as caring and justified.
- when whatever he does positively still doesn't alter the general negative image that he has, while whatever mom does negatively doesn't alter the general positive image that she has.

Once again, regardless of the many justifiable reasons for married men to be angry, they all become pathetic rationalizations because no matter the reasons, the only thing that will matter is that family members, wife, and children progressively perceive him as someone to approach gingerly or to avoid altogether. Men's focus needs to move in the direction of taking responsibility for preventing and avoiding anything in a relationship that will produce resentment, anger, and violent outbursts in him. When his negative responses occur he will get no understanding, only fear and hatred. Nobody can change that except himself and in order to do that he needs to make self-awareness and personal growth his goals because trying to make others understand his reactions is a hopeless endeavor.

The Child-Woman: Married Women who are Still Attached to Their Mothers

"Susan talks to her mother at least once a day. Whenever we have an argument or problem, she telephones her mom. As far as I can see, her mom fans the flames by being very solicitous and even encouraging her to 'come back home' for a few days instead of telling her to grow up, take some responsibility, and work things out with her husband," said Mark, who married Susan only a year earlier after an intense, highly romantic and sexual courtship of three months. "What passion," he thought initially. "She must be the soulmate I've been dreaming of but never thought I'd ever meet."

While Mark had some concerns over the fact that Susan lived on the same street as her mother and frequently went over there after work to have dinner, Mark chose to view that in a positive way. "She's a family person, loyal and caring. Obviously, she's also a good girl with old-fashioned values. It may not be trendy but it makes me feel that I can trust her," he thought. However, after living together he often heard Susan complain that she didn't feel as loved by Mark as before they were married. He was mystified when she would get tearful and call her mom to discuss her disappointment with him. The phone calls would go on for an hour or more, and it enraged Susan when she saw Mark's look of impatience over these lengthy calls. "My mom and I are close. What's wrong with that? Do you want me to be like *you* and hardly ever talk to my mother?" was Susan's irritated response.

The Dynamics of the Child-Woman

Women with a close, childlike bond to their mothers create an illusion of outward security, centeredness, and assurance that is compelling and misleading. Initially they seem to be loving and caring, as they transfer their attachment and dependence from their mother to their latest man. This love, however, alternates with hostile, even vicious outbursts as the anger they feel toward a mother who never made it possible for them to separate, and who addicted them to intense needs for closeness and attention, is transferred over to him.

Child-women are initially irresistible to men who fear demanding, dependent, intimacy-craving women. Child-women have a façade of self-confidence, strength, and inner security that comes from having been made to feel all-important, valued, needed, and protected by a mother who transferred her personal needs away from her husband and toward her daughter.

A child-woman's attractiveness stems from seemingly strong boundaries that are not a reflection of a separate identity, but of having become used to having their needs and wishes easily and quickly met, and from a sense of competence and confidence that alternates periodically with vulnerability and childlike helplessness. Child-women don't seem needy because they are used to getting instant gratification. They find men who are willing to be mother-substitutes, at least for a while.

Child-women prove to be ambivalent and full of contradictions that shake the foundations of the relationship reality. They alternate, as with their mothers, between autonomy and dependence, between childlike loving and abusive rage, as well as between feeling powerful and feeling helpless.

They are hard to read and understand, and impossible to truly become close to, because their ambivalence toward their mother is carried over in their relationship with men. They *seem* devoted and loyal, but their self-centeredness makes it impossible for them genuinely to relate to the needs of another. Their battle to achieve a separate self, and to maintain that self, creates extreme movement toward distance and detachment that disguises their childlike dependency.

Their only lasting attachment is with their mother, who has addicted them to an intensity of involvement and adoration that no man can compete with, except in the very early passionate stages of romance. So long as the child-woman remains inextricably linked to her mother in this bond, she cannot form a genuine bond with a man.

When the child-woman becomes romantically involved with a man, her mother continues to pull strings in the background. She says she wants her daughter to be in a relationship, but also wants her daughter for herself. So she subtly but systematically undermines her daughter's connection to the man, along with filling her with warnings about men because of mother's own disappointments, anger, and frustration.

The enormous seductive power that the child-woman initially has is hard for most men to resist. However, he will inevitably come to regret a relationship in which he will always fall short and never be able to fulfill his partner's standard of intimacy. The deeper cause of the trauma is the hungry and fearful masculine ego that causes men to want to be instantly the center of a woman's universe with no effort on his part. All magical illusions die in the end and trauma of the coming down far outweighs the pleasures of the going up.

Illusions of Good Mothering

A good mother is a mother who produces emotionally healthy children. She is a mother who makes it possible for the children to grow, to become fully expressive, and to separate so that they can build their own lives in their own unique ways, and who do not feel obligated, guilt-ridden, and so connected to their family to the point where they are psychologically crippled and unable to fly.

Traditional mothers participate in creating dysfunctional children in invisible ways. In the eyes of the average person, these women may appear to be wonderful, caring, selfless, and adoring. That illusion is what makes the destructive impact unstoppable as it moves along and worsens from generation to generation. They are one-half of a traditional and toxic parenting dynamic, in which the father increasingly becomes emotionally unavailable and personally disconnected from his children, creating a vacuum that unbeknownst to him, promotes his children's exaggerated attachment to the mother.

One may not criticize a woman for overmothering or for being obsessively caring. The worst criticism that is tolerated is that she worries too much, which in actuality is experienced as a compliment. What need lies behind the excess worrying is assumed to be a flaw in the right direction, when in fact, it isn't small and it isn't an error with its heart in the right place. Rather, it is at the core of one of the most damaging dynamics that a child can experience. While disconnected, workaholic, and emotionally unavailable fathers are readily identified and their hurtful impact is agreed upon, their counterpart equivalent, namely the obsessive mother, is not.

What I have observed in my years as a practicing psychologist is the enormous gap between image and reality; between what seems to be and what actually is. In the sanctified matter of mothering, the gap between what appears to be loving and positive behavior and the actual impact of an obsessive mother on a child is extreme. Yet, the cloak of loving intentions shields mothers as they participate in an ongoing generational and pathological process that progressively worsens. Children's personalities become increasingly fragmented and vulnerable. However, it is an issue that can't be readily discussed without provoking a defensive storm of accusations about men being hostile to women or blaming mothers. Confronting an obsessively fused mother about the damage she inflicts hits within a woman's denial system and a larger cultural blind spot.

In the traditional man-woman/masculine-feminine dynamic, men are held solely responsible because they act and are overt, while women react and their effect is covert. In a non-psychological world, what is not overt is not acknowledged as real. Once something is observed beyond surface appearance, and attention is directed to process (the how) rather than content (the what), the reality turns out to be opposite to what seems to be. Nowhere is that more clear than in the matter of obsessive or fusion mothering where such behavior is seen as selfless and loving, while fathers are blamed for being too distant and therefore the cause of the child's problems.

The three children of the Reynolds family were products of obsessive mothering. Mrs. Reynolds, the wife of a workaholic businessman, was seemingly a totally devoted mother. She centered her life around her children. However, even in their thirties and forties, not one of these three bright, attractive adults had managed to separate emotionally sufficiently to build and maintain a life or family of their own.

While the father was building his business empire in order to provide his family with the good life, as he chose to believe, mother knew and monitored her children's behavior. Even as adults, the ones who managed to leave the home for periods of time during an intimate relationship eventually returned to her once these relationships broke off.

These children were classic California offspring: physically attractive, warm, and intelligent. Mother fused with them because of her frustrated and intense intimacy needs. When they were young, she knew all of their friends, welcomed them into her large home, and participated in all their school functions. She befriended and praised their teachers, who returned the favor by terming her a model mother. "What a world this would be if all mothers were like you," was her favorite compliment. She smiled knowingly and made sure her children heard the remark. "You are all very lucky children," she would say. Even father had to agree because this allowed him to guiltlessly go on his disconnected way, making money and building his business. When he did have the time, mother told him he needed to just relax and enjoy himself, and leave the care of the children to her.

Only one of her children, a teenage daughter, rebelled and tried to separate. She chose drugs and died in her early twenties. None of the others could muster up any consistent resistance toward their mother in their attempts at developing a separate, private self and life. Whenever one of the children made movements toward autonomy by creating separate friendships or activities that mother was not given access to, she became punitive, guilt-making, and undermining until the children gave up trying to function autonomously.

When they were young the appearance was of a very close-knit, ideal, loved family. As they became adults, the children all became dysfunctional, and the father was blamed for never having been available. The anger and resentment the children felt for having their separate lives aborted was disguised by "nice" exteriors, while various addictions and passive-aggressive behaviors such as rarely following through with commitments became their mode. None ever accumulated enough money to support a separate residence, though periodically one of the daughters would be rescued by a protective male who was attracted to their physical beauty and "niceness." However, he would ultimately become repelled by the woman's continuing childlike dependence on mother and family and by her childlike lack of responsibility. Of course, he was blamed for being fearful of intimacy. What looked so good and close and loving in the early years became increasingly dysfunctional as they grew older.

In few matters is the disparity between image and psychological reality greater within a dynamic that has a façade that is seemingly perfect, loving, and beyond criticism, but is poisonous and destructive in its effect and impact. Rarely is it more clearly seen than in the generational transmission of obsessive mothering that looks so good to the untrained eye. It seems beyond criticism and confrontation, though it is a core part of the seed that damages children and transmits dysfunction. It prevents girls from separating and experiencing autonomous strength, eventually bringing them to depression, food addictions, and rage toward men for their "inability to love" and be "intimate." In a boy, it plants the seed of chronic sex role confusion and self-hate as he tries to become the man he doesn't feel he is.

Men who are in relationships with daughters of obsessive mothers inevitably are defeated in their attempts to make it work. He cannot be as intimate and loving as mother was. These men are never enough and are always found wanting. They may buy into the woman's interpretation that she is the love connection while he is damaged and flawed in his ability to love. He can't quite understand what is wrong, but he is sure the problem is *him*.

The Fusion Mother

Fusion mothers, an extreme variation of obsessive mothers, are those who, under the guise of great love, use their children to satisfy their own needs. They can be recognized by their undue closeness to the child to the point where mother and child become as one and the child's growth into separate, healthy adulthood is aborted. The phenomenon of fusion mothering is in part the inevitable endpoint of generations of disconnected fathers who propelled their children deeply into the arms and soul of their mothers because fathers' conditioning had severely damaged their capacity for healthy empathy and attachment to their children, while transforming them into critical, unavailable, and threatening parent figures.

Fusion mothers are difficult to identify and recognize, partially because it is politically incorrect to confront an adoring, devoted mother about her unhealthy closeness to her child. Fusion mothers are addicted to their children and react with angry denial and defensiveness when it is suggested that their attachment is damaging to the child.

The traditional relationship tends to breed fusion mothers because women in them are unhappy and frustrated with the lack of intimacy and sensual connection with their husbands. Father may be a nice guy, responsible, and respectful, but he is incapable of satisfying mother's needs. Since mother and father are intertwined, there is no appropriate place for mother to turn to get her needs met, so unconsciously she turns to her children for her gratification. She sublimates her needs through her children.

She is playing out her job in the only way that she can, given the psychological circumstances. She believes she is giving her children her all and is bewildered when their distressing dysfunctions become visible as they get older. "How come my child is so angry at me? All I ever did was love him," is her plaintive cry. She can't see her part in creating it, so she looks outside of herself for the reasons to blame. This hurts the children even more because the misidentification of external causes prevents the kind of healing and separation to take place that is needed. Instead, the children's problems are blamed on peers, the society and culture, unhealthy social values, biochemistry, genetics, or "unknown factors," anything except looking at and transforming where it all begins, namely, the nature of the bonding and attachment between mother and child.

The aware person, male or female, will define a good mother and/or good father not by surface or visible content, but by the minimal degree of defensive process that is constant, yet below the surface between parent and child. Too much parenting and love is as damaging as too little.

Because the field is bogged down by debates on the "right way" to parent, what is labeled good parenting may be unhealthy. Gang members, addicts, and dysfunctional or emotionally disturbed children can as easily come from what appear to be loving families as from so-called bad homes.

The fusion mother, who unknowingly aborts the separate identity of her children, can be defined and recognized by the degree of her preoccupation and worry about her children, and the extent to which they are the primary outlet for her needs and energies. Specifically, it is the extent to which she fuses with her children and gets her identity and validation through mothering and pulls away from everything that doesn't involve them, including her husband, which defines her unhealthy fusion.

Fathers participate in creating the fusion mother phenomenon and the no-win situation they will find themselves in. To the extent he is not available emotionally because he becomes a workaholic and compulsive provider, he is resented. To the extent he expects attention and affection and is not wholly absorbed in work and providing, he may be seen as too needy and childlike and resented even more.

Fused children tend to incorporate their mother's feelings and identify with her experiences. The frustration, blaming, and resentment she harbors—even silently—toward her husband, the children incorporate and then relate to him in kind. Often the real feelings are disguised until a crisis, such as a divorce, at which time they abandon him.

Agreements men make with their wives before a child is born regarding shared parenting and equal responsibility for working and earning *cannot* be maintained in the face of the power of this deeper current. Once the child is born, no matter what their agreement, the child will belong to her, as father progressively fades into the background, resentful but helpless to alter the course.

Early awareness is a possible preemptor. Men can recognize a woman with a fusion mother dynamic through the following signs:

- obsessiveness, manifested by prolonged attachment with the child through sleeping with the baby and nursing so long as it is only meeting mother's needs, not the child's
- a desire in her to withdraw from external commitments such as a job or career and to stay at home with the child when it is no longer necessary
- her belief that she knows what her child needs, which cannot be resisted or disputed by the father without confronting her rage
- controlling the child's experience in the real world by constructing her idea of a perfect world in which friends, activities, environment, and feelings are obsessively monitored
- instant and intense defensive anger on her part when the possibility is raised that her mothering is excessive, damaging, or intrusive
- progressively losing sexual interest in her partner and focusing instead on the needs of the child
- rage at father if he relates to the child in a way that she believes is wrong
- a rigid and defensive sense of righteousness about her mothering, which cannot be challenged or questioned because she has no doubt about her mothering behavior
- a belief that whatever problems the child has are externally caused and have little to do with her effect and impact
- continual hurt and angry feelings toward her male partner, who never seems to get it right as father or husband.

Men who remain in the relationship are certain to be defeated once enmeshed in that process. Parenting within these relationships, no matter how hard he tries or how much quality time he invests, is sure to leave him on the outside, estranged from and even disliked by his children.

Fathers may blame themselves and wonder what they did wrong. They were defeated by an invisible, unacknowledged dynamic and process. Once in it, there was no right way to correct it except to get in touch with feelings of hopelessness and to see it accurately in order to eliminate self-loathing and self-destructive behaviors.

While leaving early may trigger guilt and fear over the loss of the children, in the long run it will provide him the opportunity to establish an independent relationship with them. The longer he stays, even if it is for "their good," the more damaged and impossible his relationship with them will become.

Recognizing the undertow, acting true to how it feels, and not using external strategies and manipulations to alter the course is the way to manage and maximize an otherwise losing situation.

Some Other Reasons Things Change after the Baby Comes

The mother, whose attention and affections moves away from her partner and focuses exclusively on the baby, is like the man who withdraws after sex and turns his attention to the football game on television after he's gotten what he needs. She is turning from one fusion outlet (him) to a more satisfying and controllable one (the baby), just as he is turning from a disconnection outlet (the woman as a sex object) to a more satisfying and controllable one (the television) after sex.

Traditional psychological "wisdom" says that men who feel abandoned by their wives and feel neglected after the baby is born are simply being competitive with the baby for the wife's attention. They are told that it's only natural for women to become totally focused on the baby. While that explanation is an appealing and seeming truism, it denies the reality of the undertow and the fact that men sense the deeper shift in their relationship after the birth. The message he gets is, "I don't need you any longer. I have what I really wanted, and I feel much more fulfilled by *my* baby."

A woman who is genuinely connected to her male partner in a healthy way will experience no dramatic shift away from him and in the direction of an obsessive focus on the baby after the birth. The woman who was only going through the motions of romance with her partner because what she really wanted was to be a mother will lose interest in her partner after the child is born. Nothing has really changed. However, the hidden or denied agenda has surfaced, and is now visible.

Just as men in hot sexual pursuit of a woman change after they achieve their goal of conquest, women who are basically using a man to become mothers change after they achieve their goal of motherhood. To the extent that a man has been objectified for that purpose, that change in her can vary from benign indifference to hateful rejection of him. For men to understand this they need only reflect on the variations of their response to a woman after they have succeeded in having sex with her. To the extent to which they have used her as an object and had no interest in her as a person, the after-sex reaction may vary from an indifferent turning away to an extreme of revulsion or contempt.

The woman who changes the most after the baby comes is the woman who has most objectified the man. A man who has allowed himself to be objectified has probably unknowingly objectified the woman in return. It is easier to see what has been done to oneself than what one has done to create a painful relationship situation. It is both futile and counterproductive to complain about how the woman has changed and how he feels rejected by her after the baby comes. The challenge is to see how he invited her to use him and why, in the hopes that there is still enough to build on to create a real relationship.

Being Fathers

Mechanical Fathering: Why Quality Time Doesn't Make His Kids Bond with Him

Jim was a mechanical father. His experience with his own father, who had been unapproachable and critical, caused Jim to vow to be a completely different kind of father himself. Before his first child was born, he determined he was going to be the responsive, present, non-punitive, and supportive "perfect dad." In preparation, he read all the books and went to numerous workshops on fatherhood.

That reassured him that he could achieve a significantly different relationship with his child than he had with his own father. To his dismay, after years of seemingly doing everything right, his wife divorced him. Then, as a single parent he was shocked to discover that his child had little interest in being with him, and seemed to resist and avoid their relationship. Ultimately it got so painful to be together as his child progressively became more hostile in its response to Jim that the relationship dissolved altogether. Typical of mechanical fathers, Jim blamed both his ex-wife for poisoning the child's mind and society for denigrating fathers in children's eyes. In doing so, he missed the point, which was that his relationship with his child was created by the way he was experienced. He had been blinded to that reality by his own externalized "good fathering" intellectualizations.

Mechanical fathers do all the appropriate, responsible, and seemingly loving things expected, but it is actually disconnected behavior. Mechanical fathers are the product of externalized process which causes men to go through the motions of good or even excellent fathering, but with an endpoint result no different, if not worse, than had he been indifferent or not present at all. Indeed, the latter may have a healthier impact because the message is clean and clear and not muddled by a façade of sensitivity, which will confuse children who are trying to cope with the guilt, frustration, and anger they feel.

The totally absent father may at least get nostalgia or "longing love" from his child. Debbie, a professional woman and single mother, was raising her nine-year-old daughter by herself. The daughter had never seen her father, who had been married to another woman when he fathered the girl and denied his paternity until a DNA test legally revealed his fatherhood. Still, he refused to see his daughter out of anger toward her mother. However, at age nine, this girl was still writing letters to her father, as she had done throughout her young life, and telling him how much she loved him and wanted to meet him.

Even abusive fathers may get the love and longing of a child who still does things to try to please and win dad's approval and love. They care how the father feels, even though they are treated badly.

Contrast that with the experience of the mechanical father.

He is a good, even excellent father in his fathering behaviors, but on a deeper level, his externalization disconnects him and there is no adhesion with his child. No matter what he does, no bond is created. Because he was always there and always a good dad, he does not get the benefit of a nostalgic longing for what never was that the absent father gets, nor the approval hunger the rejecting, abusive father gets. Ironically, instead of being loved and appreciated, he may even be disliked or hated. The children view him negatively based on his externalized *process*, which causes him to come across as clueless and irritating.

Mechanical fathers focus on content and are oblivious to their process, or how they are experienced. They are focused on what they *do* as fathers, not on *how* they are experienced. As mechanical fathers, they make fathering a priority; that is, they are always there, and always involved when they're supposed to be. They go to teacher conferences, coach little league games, help with homework, and schedule themselves around their children's needs, but all to no avail. The children will experience him as well-meaning at best, but impossible, out of touch, or negative and irritating to be around at worst.

Process transforms and erodes content. That reality remains in denial until the end result clearly reveals itself. His children grow up and are uninterested in him, except for what he can do for them. It is mother they worry about, and with whom they stay connected emotionally. Because his externalization made his fathering mechanical, no deeper, emotional bond was created.

The Riddle of Dads Who are Disliked

Dads are hurt and embittered by the realization that their efforts to be good fathers have failed. In spite of having given it their best, they find themselves ignored, distanced emotionally, or disliked by their children. What went wrong?

Children embody and manifest the defensive polarization of the parental relationship. Children's responses have little to do with what a father believes he has done. A father can be a great dad in his own eyes, yet still be disliked, avoided, or reviled.

The prevailing idea is that men who make fathering a priority and are there for the children at important times, in loving, sensitive ways, and who carve out lots of quality time, will have a stronger bond with their children than fathers of the past did, and will be loved in return.

Paradoxically, the opposite is as likely to occur. A father who spends lots of time with his children may be disliked more than an absent father who doesn't because his process impact, or his psychological effect, is felt more when the child is bonded emotionally with mother. The child will experience the father the way mother does. Therefore, the greater the amount of time he spends with his child, the more he will be disliked.

Children's bond with, and feelings toward, their fathers have little to do with what the father does overtly or how *good* a father he is according to common definition. Children's feelings result from the impact of his process, and the degree of his externalization and mother's internalization. The more complete a child's fusion with mother is, the more the child's feelings will mirror the mother, *no matter what* the father does. Rejected and hated dads of past generations were probably equally shocked and dismayed at their failure to be loved by their kids.

The delusion of contemporary men who disliked and/or hated their own fathers is that their children will feel differently about them because they know how to parent, and give their children love and priority. To the extent that the change in contemporary fathers is an external or content change, and his denied process of disconnection and externalization is like that of his father, if not greater, he will have the same effect on his child as that of his dad, regardless of his good intentions. His goal focused, achievement driven, competitive, and intellectualized process or way of being is what will create the child's feelings, not his overt "good dad" behaviors.

It doesn't matter that he's an "enlightened," liberated and sensitive, well-meaning father. The children will come to feel:

- Dad is always busy and really wants to be left alone.
- Dad doesn't listen.
- Dad is impatient.

- Dad is hard to get close to.
- Dad doesn't know how to have fun.
- Dad just gives us pep talks to solve our problems; he doesn't understand and really doesn't care.
- Dad is critical of us.
- Dad has a negative attitude toward everything.
- Dad is preoccupied.
- Dad makes mother unhappy.

Some of the "best fathers" are men whom children don't like. These men all have denied masculine process beneath their modern and enlightened ideas and attitudes about parenting. They'll be surprised and even embittered by the way their children come to feel toward them in the face of their efforts to be good fathers. The child's real feelings toward dad may be masked until the child grows up, leaves home, or there is a divorce and the child has to choose. It is at that time that the absence of the loving connection with dad will be clearly manifested.

Reasons for Men not to Fight Custody Battles

A number of years ago, when I would pick up my daughter after school in the sixth grade, there was a man I would see there who was faithfully picking up his two children. He was earnest, devoted, and reliable, the personification of a caring father. He was a single dad who had custody of children who hadn't seen their mother in several years. Toward the end of the school year, I noticed that he hadn't been coming to pick up his children for several weeks, so I inquired about him from a parent who was a friend of his. I was told that their mother had recently come back to visit the kids, and after a weekend of being with her, the children, happy and excited, expressed a desire to move back with her to her home in Colorado. The father was helpless in the face of his children's pleading and urgency.

In another instance, a man had recently separated from his wife. During his marriage, this successful businessman had structured his busy work life so that he could be available to his children. They were his first priority, even though he had an engineering consulting business with 11 employees and clients all over the country. As his children became teenagers, he began to work out of his home so that he could be there for their games, PTA meetings, and at-home projects. He bought a private plane just so he could always return from business meetings in order to attend his children's games and school functions. So concerned was he about their education, he ran for and won a position on the school board. Whenever either of his two children had a problem at school, he was there to meet with their teacher, to defend them against any unfair action, and to straighten things out.

His relationship to his wife wasn't good. She was often critical of his opinions about the children and his parenting philosophy. For years she had been sexually withdrawn from him because of her many resentments. Consequently, when his youngest was 14 years old he began an affair with a prominent local businesswoman and subsequently left his wife to be with her.

What he discovered was that all the years of being there for his children and making them a priority had resulted in a "worse than nothing relationship." They didn't want to be with him. On the weekends and other times when they were in his custody, they were hostile and withdrawn, sitting silently and sullenly watching television at his apartment until it was time for them to go back to their mother. Once they passed age 18, both of his children opted to not see him at all.

While he could blame his wife for "poisoning" the children's minds and promoting the alienation, it became clear that it had little to do with her. His children just didn't like being around him. While he had been the "perfect" father in terms of his commitment, caring, and devotion, he couldn't connect with them. In their minds he was a know-it-all who lectured them and always knew the right way to do things. They disliked him and learned to tune him out.

A woman I know, who wanted a child, began dating a married man who thought she was on birth control. When he found out she was pregnant, he was enraged and withdrew from her completely. The woman, an independent professional, decided not to pursue child support because she didn't want the angry father in her life. When I met and became friendly with her and her seven-year-old daughter, I discovered that the daughter was constantly composing letters of longing to the father who lived nearby, but didn't want to see her because he felt he'd been used by the mother. Years went by, but when the father finally responded to the child's letters and messages, the girl was overjoyed. Even though she had never seen her father, when she finally met him she was excited, happy, and appreciative.

One thing that struck me most clearly and powerfully during the period when Robert Bly was a prominent father figure to the men's movement, was the recurring theme in the lives of many of the men who attended his workshops of an absent or negative connection to their fathers. Many hated the father they remembered as having been critical, abusive, alcoholic, self-centered, emotionally unavailable, controlling, angry, and pretty much impossible to talk to. Others just felt indifferent, as if they had no father at all.

Their feelings, which determined their memories of their fathers, were not that different from what feminists had been saying that these men were like. The irony, however, was that in most cases these were not absent fathers. These dads had been at home throughout. These were fathers who, I'm sure, were convinced that they had been good parents, doing the "right thing" as they believed that to be. In the end, these fathers, like my client and the Mr. Mom of my daughter's elementary school, were dumbfounded that after all they believed they had done for their children, their children could care less about them, and in many cases, even hated them.

What comes through from these examples is that the issue in fathering goes way beyond physical access to the children and loving intentions. I have no doubt that most of the fathers who now are rejected and even hated loved their children. Ironically, those who were full-time dads, still married to the mother, might actually have been appreciated more had they been at home less or gone from home entirely. To the children, the father's presence was toxic, a negative because of how he related and how he was experienced. The more he was around, the more he was disliked and avoided. It didn't matter what he thought he was trying to do as a parent. What mattered was how he came across to the children, how it felt to be with him.

How a father is experienced is usually something he can't see, any more than most men can see when they are being blatantly manipulated and used by women. Call it ego, cluelessness or denial, fathers can't see it, and children disguise their real feelings out of fear or cynical indifference and disdain. What fathers aren't aware of, however, is the real reason father-child bonds dissolve. Were the bond there, no amount of physical separation could dissolve and destroy the relationship.

How does all of this relate to custody issues and battles? These power struggles over access to the children are usually ludicrous and pathetic as two parents nitpick over the exact amount of days and times that they will spend with the children. The custody battles are misguided and redirected control and revenge battles that have nothing to do with the children, and their welfare, nor will the outcome of these battles affect the deeper relationship between the children and each parent, except for traumatizing and polarizing them. Particularly, once the child is more than three or four years old, the die has been cast. If the bond is positive and present, little will disrupt it except temporarily. If the bond is absent or negative, the custody fight will just exacerbate it. The more dad battles mom for custody, the more the children will recoil from him, as they perceive their mother as being abused. If he "wins," he will have won nothing, as any potential for positive bonding has been seriously damaged.

Looked at from another angle, in a relationship of love and attraction, whether romantic or a friendship, think about those people in your life who you were drawn to and had a warm, positive feeling toward. You may have only been with them a small amount but their memory is large and potent. Getting together is strongly anticipated. In between seeing each other, though they may not be around in person, they exist powerfully in fantasy. If it's a woman a man is attracted to, weeks and months may go by, but when she reappears it's as if no time has elapsed. Likewise with a beloved friend—years may pass without physical contact, yet the moment they are present it feels exciting and enjoyable. However, if a bond is not there or is negative, contact with the person only strengthens the resistance and dislike.

I have seen men impale themselves emotionally and financially in misguided, destructive custody battles. They are victims of a classic masculine blind spot, namely, the belief that their relationship to their children has to do with schedules, access, and not letting the mother "win" or control the children. They spend fortunes of time, money and emotion only to discover that the "victory," if accomplished, was hollow.

When children are bonded to and love a parent, even if they see the parent rarely, they will be excited and happy when they are with them. In between they will be anticipating, longing, and thinking about them. On the other hand, I've seen men who gain joint or full custody in the courts, only to discover that the weekends or times when they have them, their child doesn't want to be with them and is hostile, withdrawn, and passive-aggressive. It becomes so painful and "impossible" to be together that eventually they give up. It's not very enjoyable to be with a child who makes it clear that he doesn't like you and doesn't want to be with you—or worse, to be with a child who sees it as punishment to be with dad.

Growth for fathers means to gain awareness of how it is for the child to be with them, rather than fighting for their "right" to parent. It is traditionally masculine to turn a relationship problem into an issue of "right" and "wrong," or a battle over rights. However, it is my belief that a protracted custody battle, and the perception that the courts discriminate against men and prevent them from being fathers, is largely delusional and a final nail in the relationship coffin for men.

If a child wants to be with his father and the mother blocks or prevents it, the outcome will be that the child will resent the mother and make mother's life hell until she gladly gives the child over to the father. If the child doesn't want to be with dad and no positive bond or connection exists, even if mom is supportive of the child's relationship with him, the experience will be negative.

There are many psychological reasons why an ugly custody battle, particularly one in which a man believes that he is fighting the system and the poisonous influence of the mother over his children, is counterproductive and damaging to a man's expressed desire to parent his progeny. The following are some of them:

- By the end of a marriage, a woman's rage over feeling she has been controlled and abused is at a peak. She sees custody issues as the final battleground and will relentlessly fight to any extreme in order to win. Attorneys feed on this adversarial tone and see it as a way to make money as they stoke the rage. She will pull out all stops, and drain the father and both of their finances in this final stand to not let him get his way "this time."

- In most families, children have a stronger emotional connection to their mother. In painful custody battles, because the children are vulnerable and threatened, they will bond even more strongly with her and will perceive what father is doing through the mother's eyes. Whereas a man may believe his children will appreciate how hard he is fighting for the right to be with them, he is wrong. What the child sees is that dad is abusing mother.

- If a man has a loving bond already in place with his child, the child will miss him. A mother who blocks the child's ability to be with him will find her life made hellish by an angry and rebellious child.

- A woman is energized by a custody battle with the father. It is her chance to "pay him back" for years of feeling and believing that she has been diminished and abused. Without such a battle to engage in, it is very likely that mom won't even want that much responsibility or time with the children. She'll focus instead on her need for freedom, the opportunity to enjoy herself and to act on what she believes are her long-suppressed impulses. She may in fact try and push the children onto their father so that she can be free to date, be with another man, or pursue her newfound passions.

- Even in the worst-case scenario, where a man is denied contact with his children altogether, if a positive bond is in place, it will remain and grow in memory. His influence will remain, as the child will do things to make dad proud in the future. Once the child enters their teens or young adulthood, he or she will seek out the father and the intervening years of no contact will dissolve.

- Fighting custody battles only promotes a masculine nightmare of personal and relationship disconnection. Relationships are not about control, power, winning, or losing. They are about emotional connection, empathy, and bonding. A man's energy should go toward personal transformation to develop ways to maximize his connection to his child and overcome his relationship shortcomings. To do that, he must first acknowledge them and overcome his belief that he is a maligned, but good and loving father who isn't dysfunctional, but is being abused and misunderstood.

- As a working therapist for many years, I've never seen a man benefit from fighting these battles. Even if he wins in court, he has won the battle, yet lost the struggle to focus on and nurture his bonding potential.

- Relationships with one's children are continually in flux and no court can nail that down. Whatever it is today, it will be something different tomorrow. Court-made agreements are washed away each time the tide turns.

7 What Men Still Don't Know About Transforming Their Relationships

✓ Why Content Solutions to Process Problems Don't Work

✓ Making Issues Out of Relationship Problems

✓ Making It Work: The Best-Case Scenarios

✓ The Real Loving Woman

✓ Guidelines for Understanding and Managing Relationships

Why Content Solutions to Process Problems Don't Work

"How to" advice given to couples to solve their problems is not just wrong, it can lead to despair about ever "getting it right" and to a premature giving up on the relationship. Simply put, it leads to the feeling of "We've *tried* everything and nothing works. We're just not right for each other."

Couples who believe they have tried *everything* have only done so on a content level, and content solutions cannot remedy process-created problems that occur due to polarization and the defensive overreactions, distortions, and rigidities they generate.

If a woman's low self-esteem comes from the fact that she has unconsciously rendered herself "helpless" by being a reactor rather than an actor, and an accommodator who doesn't draw boundaries in her need to be "nice" and to avoid conflict and disagreements, the content solution of bolstering her self-esteem by having her partner say positive, supportive things to her, buying new clothes, or her losing weight, won't work, even though they may create a temporary, misleading "feel good" moment.

The effect of content solutions, like all temporary escapes, will fade and the ongoing process-generated feelings of low self-esteem will return. Each time they do, they will be accompanied by a greater sense of pessimism and hopelessness about ever really getting a lasting solution. For the woman with low self-esteem due to her reactive, accommodating process, there will always be something to make her feel criticized, put down, or triggered to not feel good about herself, until the denied process behind her experience is identified, acknowledged, and altered.

Deeper relationship feelings are generated by relationship process, not by its content. A man may do everything right (content) and still alienate his wife and children if his process is one of seeming to be emotionally unavailable, uninterested, or controlling, all of which he is probably in denial of. The faithful, hardworking, responsible, and caring father all-too-often discovers that in spite of having lived up to the image of being a good husband and father, his wife is unhappy and blames him for her feelings, while his children have no feelings of closeness to him.

If a man feels bored, smothered, and irritable in a relationship because he is disconnected in his process, causing him to have no capacity for personal interactions or awareness of his own feelings, nothing beyond momentary excitement and external stimulation and distraction will cause him to feel connected, interested, and happy about personal interaction. Content solutions, such as leaving him alone, not interfering while he's watching sports or paying his bills, giving him space, or doing exciting things, will be no more than a temporary fix. His ongoing deeper response, caused by his denied and defensive externalized process, will continue to return, causing those around him who tried to make him feel better to give up trying. By trying to solve his problems with external, logically created remedies, he will ultimately decide that it's no use trying to relate and feel close. The attempts to change matters by using content solutions will only make things worse by generating false hopes, which are then repeatedly dashed until they grind things down to a level of giving up.

The answer, which involves working to alter his process, may occur to him after it is too late and loved ones have abandoned him. At that point, it might occur to him that it was *how* he was to be with, and not anything specific that he had done, that caused his personal downfall.

If a woman continuously feels attacked and abused because of a man's harsh and insensitive impact, and it causes her to want everything to be "nice," and to cry and become defensively overreactive when things aren't, no matter how he tries to change and be gentle with her, it won't work. Even when there is no obvious cause, she will find something to construe as hostile, hurtful, or abusive, even if that turns out to be an innocent or playfully intended comment or joke on his part. Nothing short of her identifying and acknowledging her overt but denied power, and learning to express and be comfortable with that part of herself, will make any difference in her process-created problem.

Similarly, the common "how to" advice about couples needing to take time to "really listen to each other," to "really try and communicate," and to carve out quality time to do something romantic in order to breathe life into a deadened interaction will fail because the miscommunication and the boredom and the misinterpretations between them are not due to a lack of "trying." They are byproducts of a polarized process that produces a different interpretation of identical events for both. She may experience him as not caring when he really does, while he may see her as being pressuring and emotionally out of control when she really isn't, or is simply being triggered into a response of desperation by his emotional detachment. If they follow "how to" advice, they will come to feel hopeless.

Likewise, she might feel a lack of romance and intimacy because, unknowingly, she longs for a fusion that can never exist between two functional adults, or he might feel an absence of sexual excitement because his lack of personal involvement has created a need for intense, fantasy-ridden sexual stimulation to replace his emotional and personal deadness. Only a manipulative, ego-feeding, sexual novelty rather than a relationship can fill that "need" and "turn him on." Until his process is changed so that he can find pleasure in closeness and not just erotic stimulation, all the "how to" efforts to arouse him sexually will become progressively less stimulating until he finds himself unable to be aroused at all. The "cause" is him, it is not "out there."

In all these instances, "how to" content solutions will only lead to the despair that comes from having done everything the experts suggested, and seeing it not to be effective.

Starting Over: Their Reciprocal Contributions

There is no change without awareness of our own defensiveness, anxiety, discomfort, and confusion over changing something that generally reassures us. The tendency is to seek shortcuts and a panacea in the form of:

- Information and advice.
- Trying: giving the other person what they say they want.
- Attitude change: "not being sexist," or "lightening up," and "having a sense of humor" or a "positive attitude."

In a polarized relationship, the above are useless. They represent the beginning of the end because they are efforts to create content solutions to process-created problems. More than anything else, starting over requires identifying and holding onto the elusive thread of process, in which a man and a woman focus primarily on how they are experienced by their partner, as opposed to what they do or intend. While initially threatening, it is the soil of relationship growth and genuinely good feelings.

Making Issues out of Relationship Problems

Making issues out of relationship problems is the product of intellectualization and the denial of the effect of one's own process. The feminists made an issue out of sexism, the ways society held them back and denied them opportunity, power, and reward, and how men used and abused them sexually. All these contentions were plausible on the surface, but revealed a process distortion when examined closely. Passion for and commitment to fighting the issue, rather than a focus on how our own process creates our experience, is a guarantee of rigidifying defensiveness, aborting growth, and creating crazy-making relationship experiences where it becomes increasingly impossible to separate out what is being done to one, versus how much of it is simply blaming others for one's effect.

There are many women who have never been anybody's victims and never will be. Nobody stands in their way. They are clear about who they are, what they want, and the responsibility they have in getting it.

Men who see society as "screwing them over" are cut from the same victim cloth. When they say that society discourages men from having close friends, forces men to take responsibility for women, prevents men from putting a priority on being fathers or from expressing feelings and vulnerabilities, or rewards men for being macho and punishes the sensitive ones, they are equally in denial of their own fear of change and the process reality in which men are creating the very experiences they feel victimized by.

If society rewards men who are macho, they are rewarding self-destructiveness. The more macho his process, the more rigid, defensive, out of touch, out of control, and self-destructive a man is. Teenage males who are macho stand the best chance of early death through violence, recklessness with drugs or alcohol, foolish risk-taking, or engaging in competitive, senseless encounters. The rewards of not being macho are the built in byproducts of self care, as are the rewards of having friends, being an involved father, or not taking responsibility for women.

Society has never stopped men from being good fathers who bond with their children, or having close friends or showing their feelings. Only masculine externalization and disconnection does that. Changing oneself involves the difficult work of breaking through rigid masculine defensiveness. The disconnected male *cannot* bond with his children, and nothing society does will change that.

Making issues out of personal problems trades long-range change and growth for the short-term exhilaration of escape from responsibility and oneself, and the righteous vindication that comes from blaming mythical others.

When issues are made out of process-created problems, a person is in danger of denying one's own part in creating the experience, blaming others, and becoming rigidly defensive and cloaked behind self-righteous intellectualizations.

Making It Work: The Best-Case Scenarios

The overriding reality: The content of a relationship is the illusion and the hope. The process is what creates the experience and reality that repeats itself endlessly and defeats us ultimately, unless it is surfaced, acknowledged, worked on, and transformed.

In the best-case scenarios, men and women recognize the overwhelming power of traditional masculine and feminine process to shape and poison their relationship experiences, and they join together in a non-blaming effort to grow beyond each of their own defensive processes.

In best-case scenarios, men and women can acknowledge their own process blind spots and defenses when these are pointed out. They reach out to each other for feedback and encouragement as they confront the elusive and difficult task of change, which cannot be done alone in a relationship. Men need help to overcome their fear that change will lead to humiliation, vulnerability, powerlessness, and rejection. Women need help to overcome their fear that change will lead to a loss of safety, security, and the relationship power that comes from being reactive and feeling like a victim.

The price for not changing in order to avoid the anxiety of the unknown is the inevitable impossibility of male-female closeness and love, with men locked into compulsive performing, achieving, and proving, and women locked into patterns of increasing relationship obsessiveness and frustration, the loss of identity boundaries, the fear that comes from feeling powerless in the world, and the pain of unfilled intimacy need.

The Real Loving Woman

There are some women who, by virtue of the work they've done on themselves or the healthy role models their parents provided, raise the potential of a relationship. With these women, even though relationship issues and problems come up, the way they respond and negotiate will allow for growth rather than polarization to occur. Some of the identifying characteristics of these women are listed. The caveat is that the real loving woman is one part of the necessary, healthy foundation that allows a positive relationship to build, but by herself she is not the solution. She is one part of a beginning toward a real and loving experience. He is the other part.

How to Recognize the Real Loving Woman

- She knows herself well enough to separate out her responsibility for a problem from her partner's. When there's conflict, she first reflects on her part, not yours.
- When there's an argument or problem, the dialogue is free of blaming and guilt.
- Sex is easy, just another part of a relaxed and pleasurable interaction.
- She knows her partner as he knows himself, not as she imagines or wants him to be. She loves the person he knows himself to be.
- When she speaks, his mind is fully present, because she speaks *to him*, not to herself with him as a witness.
- She responds to what he says, the way he intended, and not her interpretation of what he intended.
- When she confronts him on his flaws, he doesn't feel attacked. What she says makes sense. It's not a distortion or a projection, and so he wants to hear it.
- What she gives to him or does for him is directly in line with what he wants, not with what she believes he should want.
- When he gives her input or feedback, she welcomes it and doesn't experience it as an attack or a criticism.
- When she talks about being intimate, it has to do with being close to him, rather than simply needing him to reduce her anxiety about being abandoned or for reassurance.
- When making love, he never thinks of his performance, but of being close and loving to her.
- She doesn't expect him to always be "nice." Rather, she wants him to be genuine.
- She wants to know how he experiences her and can listen to his experience non-defensively.

Identifying and Overcoming the Obstacles to Being with the Real

Loving Woman

For most men, the primary obstacle to finding a real loving woman is being initially attracted and choosing a woman based on how she looks and how she makes a man feel about himself, rather than how she is to be with. By choosing women based on their physical features, men almost certainly make the experience of being with a real loving woman impossible. The reason is simple: By doing so, a man has set in motion a process of objectification. While women and men both tend to invite objectification out of insecurity, fear, and gender defensiveness, being objectified inevitably produces a buildup of resentment and an endpoint of rage. Therefore, for a man to bring into his life the ongoing experience of a real loving woman, he needs to have worked through his own externalized gender process and his need for an instant romantic and sexual connection.

In objectified relationships the "best" comes first, followed by a progressive decline. While a man's experience of the real loving woman does not occur with the accompanying excitement of an addictive fix, it grows slowly to an experience that is both deeply satisfying and founded in the reality of two persons, rather than the fantasy of two perfect objects. Even if the relationship does not work perfectly or survive, it will never produce the trauma and rage that are the byproducts of the traditional objectified relationship where the woman is a temporary fantasy who can never be transformed into the genuine reality of a loving partner.

Guidelines for Understanding and Managing Relationships

- Never act or make decisions in a relationship based on an impulse or overpowering emotion. The impulse will subside and the emotion will change, and you will be left responsible for the decision you made or the action you took.
- When you're feeling desperate about a relationship, you're either misreading it, being rejected, or being manipulated. Healthy relationships do not create out-of-control or desperate feelings.

- All relationship problems are two-way streets. If
  you feel primarily guilty or responsible, you're being
  manipulated. In the same vein, if you're feeling yourself
  to be the victim, you're not seeing your part in creating
  the problem.
- A relationship with a woman who blames you for
  its problems cannot grow and will most assuredly
  deteriorate into a nightmare of emotional explosions.
  A healthy relationship is known by its lack of blaming
  and guilt.
- When a woman is rejecting you and doesn't need you,
  you can hardly do anything right; when she wants you,
  you can hardly do anything wrong.
- If a woman "falls is love" with you when her life
  is in trouble, her feelings toward you will change
  dramatically when that trouble dissipates. Women
  become intensely romantic when they are most in
  need of being rescued, and those feelings readily turn
  to hostility when women feel they won't get what they
  want, or they no longer need it.
- For women, romance is an unconscious holiday from
  their fear and anger toward men.
- "What did I do wrong?" is rarely the correct question
  in trying to understand your relationship. You'll drive
  yourself crazy trying to figure out the answer that
  way. It's not *what* you did that created the relationship
  problems, it's the *process*, or *how*, of the interaction that
  creates its deeper feelings. You'll never find the answer if
  you focus on the *content* or the *what*.
- Relationships that happen quickly and easily are based
  on fantasy and will go into major crisis just as quickly.
  Authentic relationships, given the differences in men
  and women's process, develop unevenly and slowly.
  The higher the initial romantic high and the fantasy of
  a magical connection, the deeper and more painful the
  final crash will be.

- Because of the actor/reactor dynamic of male/ female relationships, the inevitable endpoint of every traditional relationship is an angry woman and a guilt-ridden man. Specifically, a woman with a sense of righteous blaming and of having been abused, and a man with self-hatred and guilt over feeling responsible.
- In relationships, it doesn't matter what you intend or mean; it only matters how you are experienced. A woman's reality is a logical starting point for a man's "understanding."
- Never try to reason a woman out of her feelings, and never try to use detached logic to explain yourself. It will only intensify her anger because she will experience you as distancing and defensive.
- Allowing a woman to be abusive by accusing you and raging at you is not a form of loving her. Set boundaries demanding self-respect and hold them. If the relationship has substance, it will improve. If it is contingent on unhealthy dynamics for its survival and lacks substance, setting boundaries will cause the relationship to fall apart and die.
- If you feel the need to always do things for her and to spend money in order to hold and please her, you are in a bottomless well where it will never be enough.
- After commitment, particularly marriage, the power shifts to the woman and everything changes because she now has the security to become critical and blaming of you and to allow deeper real feelings to be expressed.
- The prognosis for a relationship in trouble is in direct proportion to each person's ability to see their part in creating its problems. If one partner sees him- or herself as abused and victimized and blames the other, no real change or deeper improvement can be expected.
- Listen carefully to the way she describes the men in her past. That is how you will be described. In relationships, history repeats itself. It is a masculine delusion that you

can love her better than the men before and that she
will treat you differently than she did her past lovers. If
she cheated to be with you, it is highly probable that she
will cheat on you eventually as well.

- When a woman says you're the best lover she's ever
  had, your ego is being stroked. Sex is rarely the kind of
  experience that women can compare men on. Sexual
  excitement comes from her feelings and fantasies about
  you, not from your prowess. If the feelings are there, she
  will experience you as a wonderful lover, and if they're
  not, there's little you will be able to do to excite her.

- Women crave closeness to the same degree that men
  crave space and freedom. Intimacy is a feminine
  euphemism for fusion craving designed to quell her
  tensions, just as freedom and space are masculine
  euphemisms for the disconnection a man needs to quell
  his tensions. Each partner needs to take responsibility of
  the insatiability of their need and not blame the other.

- If she talks about wanting to be intimate, ask yourself
  if that means that you can be fully honest about your
  feelings and still be loved. If the answer is "no," her
  concept of intimacy may have more to do with the
  fulfillment of her needs and not with being close to the
  real you.

- A liberated woman can be known by how she relates,
  not on what her intellectual ideals or attitudes about
  relationships are. Toxic feminism is composed of
  liberated ideology combined with traditional process
  and the resulting irresolvable binds that they create. A
  healthy relationship in the face of these contradicting
  elements may be impossible.

- Just because a woman has a career does not mean that
  she does not want to be rescued and provided for, nor
  does it mean that she won't want to give up her career
  once she's in a committed relationship.

- Here is a major craziness or paradox in relationships: If

you don't try to satisfy a woman's needs, you arouse her frustration and anger. If you do try to satisfy her needs, you may arouse her contempt or irritation because you will fail and she will see how hopeless things are. Therefore, it is better for her to fantasize what might be if you only tried (hope remains) than for you to try and inevitably fail.

- Women objectify men according to their power symbols, just as men objectify women according to their physical symbols.
- Women have no greater genuine capacity for love than men do. It only seems that they do because their focus on relationships and personal closeness is usually greater than men's.
- You can have everything in common with a woman, but it will mean nothing if the process of the relationship is polarized. Polarized process erodes and destroys the best content and causes every relationship to seem and feel like the same frustrating ones of the past.

The major obstacle and most difficult challenge in pursuit of a genuinely loving and caring relationship is to overcome the seductive powers and the addiction to the content approach to entering, creating, and maintaining it. The elusive golden thread of understanding lies in the *how*, and not the *what*. Specifically, as gender polarization in a relationship decreases, the experience of it improves. Without that rebalancing, even the most perfect content will unravel increasingly. Once the process is balanced, the magic of having ideal content is no longer necessary. The rebalancing process which creates a relationship free of polarizing gender defenses is clearly difficult and threatening initially in the same way that giving up an addiction seems to be. Once achieved however, a relationship free of distortion, false illusions, resentment, and hopelessness truly becomes possible.